Hollywood Walk Of Crime

Edward Anderson

To my sister, Sarah Kew

CHAPTER ONE

Brothers Share And Murder Movie Star

What happens when a movie star is no longer in the movies? Some move over to directing or turn to TV to continue working. However, in Old Hollywood, they would often go into seclusion, never heard from again. Nobody wanted to see an aging lothario or starlet they had once idolized looking old on camera.

Ramon Novarro lived that life. After he was no longer considered sexy, he was discarded like so many before and after him. The Latin lover who had heated up the screens with beautiful leading ladies on-screen scorched his bedsheets with men off-screen. Unlike some leading men, the fact that he was gay did not seem to affect his career. Some argue it added to his appeal.

Meeting His Killers

Novarro had taken to hiring young men to come over to his house after his retirement in 1968. Sometimes, the men would engage in sex, but they would sit with him and have a conversation more often than not. Novarro was desperately lonely, and some say he was not ready to retire. He needed human contact.

Paul Ferguson got Novarro's number from one of the men who had visited him. They set up an appointment for Paul and his younger brother, Tom, to visit. Perhaps the intention was just for conversation, or the younger man, Paul was 22 and Tom was 17, may have promised the older man a threesome. A fantasy straight out of a porn flick. Whatever the case, the date was set.

And the countdown to Novarro's death had unexpectedly begun.

Drinking Buddies

On October 30, 1968, the Fergusons showed up at Novarro's place. As he often did with his young male companions, the retired movie star shared his liquor with them and reminisced about old times. After showing them a photograph of himself when he starred in Ben-Hur, Paul informed the older man that the picture looked nothing like him.

More booze was poured. At some point, Paul coerced Novarro to call an agent to set up an appointment for him. Afterward, the two men had sex. It is believed that they went quite a few rounds, and at some point, a horny Tom joined them in bed. After their threesome, the Fergusons wanted something more from Novarro.

There was a rumor he kept a lot of money stashed in his home, and they wanted all of it.

Murder and Coverup

Paul demanded to know where the money was. Novarro denied having a large sum of money in his home. The denial did nothing to persuade the brothers, and they began beating the movie icon. First, they used their fists. And when Novarro started to lose consciousness, they slapped him with cold water to keep him awake.

At some point, they switched to beating the older man with his cane. As Novarro lay dying on his bed, the younger men went through his belongings, tossing his photographs on the floor. Once the boys realized they had murdered Novarro, they tried to cover the crime up.

In a failed attempt at blaming members of the opposite sex, the boys wrote on the mirror: "Us girls are better than fagits (sic)." It was not hard for the police to track down the Fergusons and charge them with the murder.

Trial By Media

As was often the case in Old Hollywood, and in this particular era, the defense put the victim on trial. They tried to use Novarro's homosexuality, and lifestyle as a reason for the Fergusons murdered him. Like with his career, it did not work. The defense kept changing the motives and rationales for the horrific crime.

The young men were convicted of First-Degree Murder. Both were sentenced to life in prison, with the Judge recommending they never be released. Tom Ferguson would spend just 6 years behind bars, his brother only 9 years for the murder of Novarro. Both were paroled, many believe, because of the homophobic ideals at the time.

Both Fergusons are back behind bars for rape, separately, among other crimes. This time they are not likely to be released from jail.

CHAPTER TWO

Unsolved Murder David Bacon

The Birth Of Bacon

In 1914, David Bacon was born Gaspar Griswold Bacon Jr. Bacon's family was full of politicians. His grandfather, Robert Bacon, was Secretary of State under Teddy Roosevelt. His father served as the President of the Massachusetts State Senate and as Lieutenant Governor. Because of their status, Bacon enjoyed a life of luxury and power.

Bacon went to Deerfield Academy and then to Harvard like his grandfather. Both schools saw the scion become popular with the staff and students alike. At Harvard, Bacon even acted alongside John Roosevelt, the son of President Franklin Roosevelt. The two would become good friends during their time at school.

After he graduated from Harvard, Bacon had a life planned out for him. But there was an emptiness that his preplanned life couldn't fill. There was a siren call from New York and ultimately California that needed to be answered.

Moving To The City

The summer after he graduated, Bacon left the life he knew behind. Rumors have swirled that his family had found out that he was gay and tried to force him into conversion therapy. Other reports state he simply wanted to get away from the shadow of his family. In either case, he ended up in NYC shortly after graduation.

Stories abound the city about David Bacon, especially among the older demographic of gay men, about him selling his body for money and drugs flow. While he was never charged with solicitation, it is believed that he left with no money from his family and very few skills, even with the degree from Harvard.

He shared an apartment with two Hollywood icons, who were also on their way up the fame ladder; Jimmy Stewart and Henry Fonda. There have been rumors about a possible relationship between Bacon and Fonda but nothing substantial.

Lovers Or Friends
Howard Hughes owned RKO Films and agreed to a meeting with Bacon. This meeting was partly because of Bacon's last name and powerful connections to the elite. It has also been said that there was a more nefarious reason for it: lust.

Whatever happened at the initial meeting, no one knows for sure. Except that Bacon was signed to a deal with Hughes, and the two became very close. Some speculated there was a romance happening between the two, while others insist it was strictly professional.

Bacon and Hughes were seen having lunch and dinner together quite often. They would say they were strategizing his career. To that end, Bacon ditched his first name in favor of David, since it was pronounceable for the public. They also agreed that Bacon needed to get married. So he found Grace Keller, an opera singer. Before she died, she revealed that her marriage to Bacon had been a ruse to hide the fact they were both gay.

After the news of his marriage hit, Bacon was cast in Two Men From West Point. Even as they said he was weird, the cast praised the young actor and would often talk to himself about the dialogue. Audiences appreciated his efforts, and his career took off.

Masked Marvel Curse

Hughes loaned out his rising star to Republic Pictures. They were filming a 12 part serial called The Masked Marvel, and executives had high hopes for the series. Hughes was convinced this was the vehicle to launch Bacon into the stratosphere, even if he was the fifth choice to play the role.

Accidents befell all four actors who had taken on the role before Bacon. One day he was joking with his costars and said: "I better look out or something might happen to me." And in a moment of what could only be called an eery premonition, he predicted how he would die. "I'll probably get hurt going home in my car tonight."

It was not that night that he would be hurt in his car, but the fact he was murdered in his car makes the statement that much more powerful.

Murder On The Road

Keller became pregnant right after she and Bacon got married. Though it was hardly a time of joy. The pregnancy proved difficult, and she was put on bed rest. One fateful Saturday afternoon, Bacon had talked about going to the beach. Instead, both took a nap; when Bacon woke up, he headed out to the beach; alone.

Or was he? Multiple sources have said they saw him with another man. This mysterious man was said to have dark brown hair, though no other description was given. Some have also claimed that there was also a woman in the car. However, police have debunked that theory.

At some point in time, while on his way home, Bacon was stabbed.

"Help me, please help me!" He cried after his car careened into a bean field he stepped out of the vehicle, bleeding everywhere. A gentleman nearby urged the star to hold on, but by the time the paramedics got there, David Bacon was dead.

What Was The Motive For Murder

One of the first things that the police tried to figure out was a motive. They quickly ruled out robbery as a reason Bacon was killed. There was no money or valuables taken from him. Many people looked at blackmail as a genuine possibility; he had enough secrets to fuel the theory. Still, others simply believed, and there was a murder for hire plot.

A naked picture of Bacon on the beach is among the only pieces of evidence that survived the crash. The image was alleged to have been part of the theory that supported him being blackmailed. The picture deepened the mystery of what had happened to Bacon and why.

Also adding to the confusion was the fact the only Bacon's fingerprints were found in his car. Somehow the other passenger seemed to have vanished without leaving any kind of clue, except for one.

A blue sweater was found in the backseat of the car. It was a size too small for Bacon. Investigators believed they finally had a break. But the lead would go nowhere.

Witness To Nothing

As the police tried to unwind the mystery of who killed Bacon, another twist was about to drop. His cousin found a handwritten will in the myriad of papers on his desk. The choice, unsurprisingly, left everything to Keller. Some wondered why he wouldn't have gone to a lawyer, though. Especially since he believed his life was in danger.

Adding to the mystery; It was discovered that Bacon had a secret apartment. Police found a key for it in his wallet. When they went to search it, they found dirty dishes and food last its expiration date. A talk with the landlord proved to be fruitful, though.

According to the landlord's testimony, Bacon shared the apartment with a shorter, dark-haired man. What's more, is that the men had been arguing a day before Bacon was killed. It was an excellent lead for them to go on.

Or so they thought. The man was never found.

Hughes Accused

Weeks after Bacon was murdered, Keller delivered a stillborn baby. The double whammy sent her into a deep sadness that kept most people at bay. As she grieved her husband and her baby, she kept making an accusation that nobody paid attention to. She alleged that Howard Hughes was behind Bacon's Murder.

The story, as she told it, was that Bacon and Hughes were lovers. At some point, Bacon decided he'd had enough and no longer wanted to be with Hughes. Of course, the billionaire was angry at the rejection.

Hughes hires a hitman to take care of his dirty work, Keller alleged. After the breakup, Hughes was determined to keep the affair a secret. He didn't want someone else to get a hold of the information about his romance with Bacon.

Someone who had a contentious with Bacon lurked in the background; almost certainly, they killed him. Possibly this person even blackmailed the rising star.

Bacon's Blackmail Exposed

Bacon's homosexuality had to be hidden. It was Hollywood in the first golden age of film, and the LGBTQ community was not yet accepted by the majority of society. If someone was blackmailing Bacon, he would have been forced to pay the price by himself.

Adding fuel to the blackmail theory was Keller lying and saying that the other man in the apartment was their gardener. Police debunked this very fast. Neighbors who overheard the men arguing insisted that two lovers were fighting, not a boss/mentor having a disagreement.

After the investigation dragged on for weeks, Keller told another story. She relayed how the roof of Bacon's Cadillac was slashed. She also revealed that the story of when and how it happened kept changing all the time.

It was just another point in a story that confounded police. Bacon had lived a double life but had it led to his death. Or was Hughes just upset that the younger man broke off the relationship? Either situation is possible.

The LAPD is also still looking into the case. "It is an open case. At this time, [we] are not commenting any further."

Maybe one day, this cold case will be solved. Though since many of the significant players are deceased, it doesn't seem likely.

CHAPTER THREE

Fake News And Hollywood Love Triangle

Thomas Ince changed Hollywood forever. After getting an unsuccessful start as a stage actor, the innovative man moved to Hollywood with his wife. He implemented changes in the production system that are still used today. When he wasn't starting studios, like Paramount, that have shaped pop culture for generations.

Even so, Ince saw his fortunes dwindle, and he wanted to ensure his family would be taken care of. As such, he made moves to get out of the businesses with some money in his pocket. He began negotiations with William Randolph Hearst. The publishing tycoon would take control of Paramount, and Ince would advise him.

Before the deal could be formalized and days before his 42nd birthday, Ince would die. Leaving a very complicated mystery behind.

The Guest List
November 16, 1924, and the Hearst yacht, The Oneida, was sailing across the Pacific Ocean. A birthday dinner in Ince's honor was thrown. Hearst seemed cheerful, but he had his eye on his mistress, Marion Davies. Something was amiss, and Hearst had an idea about what it was.

He suspected that she and fellow guest, Charlie Chaplin, were far more than platonic friends. Whispers around town had made their way to him, and Hearst was now trying to find out if the rumors were true. Helping him with this bit was eventual gossip maven (though at this point in time, she was a movie critic) Louella Parsons.

Rounding out the guest list was actress Elinor Glynn.

Thomas Ince would soon leave the yacht. But confusion reigns as to why he left. Was he ill, or had he been killed?

Lies And Consequences

A big part of the reason why confusion has come out of Ince's death is its immediate aftermath. A physician aboard the yacht, Dr. Goodman, said the young mogul was suffering from indigestion and left the boat to be treated on land. The official cause of death was listed as heart failure. Yet, the Los Angeles Times had a headline declaring Ince had been shot. That headline and others like it would soon be pulled, never to be seen again.

Hearst and his newspapers claimed Ince had never been aboard the yacht. This was quickly disproven, as many people had seen him with the group. Add to that, a secretary for Hearst claimed she saw Ince bleeding from the head, and chaos controlled the narrative.

Further leading to speculation about what happened was that Ince's body was cremated before an investigation could be conducted. Nell Ince, Thomas's widow, left for Europe shortly after that.

The Coverup

The rumors were too loud for the prosecutors to ignore. So they opened an inquiry into the death of Thomas Ince. However, they only called one witness: Dr. Goodman. He stuck to the story of indigestion, and they accepted it. Many wondered why they wouldn't look further into the case. The answer was simple: the body had been cremated, leaving no evidence there. And it was an open secret that there was booze on the yacht. Since Prohibition was still in effect, they would have had to charge Hearst with having alcohol. Something nobody wanted to do.

For his part, Hearst seemed to throw around his money and influence. It is believed he gave Nell Ince a nice stipend and allowance for her to go to Europe. As it goes, the money would continue to flow for her as long as she never returned to the United States.

Shortly after the yacht incident, Louella Parsons was gifted with a lifetime contract with Hearst newspapers. This would be in effect as long as she never mentioned what happened the night Ince died. Parsons would develop a reputation for being on the pulse of breaking news, and many believe this is where it began for her.

The Night In Question

What really happened the night Thomas Ince died? Most people believe that Hearst caught Charlie Chaplin and Marion Davies in the throes of passion. Hearst marched to his room to get his gun. Davies screamed, drawing the attention of the other guests.

Hearst was startled and shot Ince instead of Chaplin, the intended target. Nobody believes Hearst shot his friend on purpose. Adding further fuel to the theory is that the tycoon would blanch whenever someone mentioned Thomas Ince in his presence.

The mystery of Thomas Ince's death will go down the canals of Hollywood's biggest mysteries and scandals.

CHAPTER FOUR

Fashionable Nazi Spy

Coco Chanel single-handedly revolutionized the fashion industry. When she suggested every woman needed a little black dress, sales skyrocketed for the staple. Then she created a perfume that remains one of the best selling scents to this day, Chanel #5.

What many don't know is that Coco Chanel is a true rags to riches story. At the age of 12, her parents sent her to the convent/orphanage. With a fierce determination, she rose through the ranks. As World War I came to an end, she was determined to show her fashion line. She succeeded. The money problems that had plagued her youth were distant memories. Replaced with a fabulous life.

But it came with a price.

The High Cost Of Success
Because of her newfound stature, she was hobnobbing with legends like Pablo Picasso and Winston Churchill. The life she had built for herself was over the top, and there was no way she wanted to go back to poverty.

As World War II loomed, she had to decide how to keep the good times rolling. The perfect opportunity dropped into her lap as she met and romanced Baron Hans Günther von Dincklage, a Nazi soldier. The relationship allowed her to move into the Paris Hotel Ritz and stay connected to high society as she wanted.

Chanel was also concerned about her nephew Andre Palasse. He was being held in a German Stalag. She worked against the clock to save him. It appears as though she was able to.

However, not all of her motives were driven by family devotion. Adolf Hitler was forcing Jewish people to divest their businesses. The Wertheimers, a Jewish family, had backed her perfume line in 1924. They did so with the agreement that they would receive the majority of the profits from the perfume business. Chanel saw this as the perfect opportunity to get control of her line back and pocket more of the profits.

Welcome Westminster

Dincklage introduced Chanel to another high ranking agent, Baron Louis de Vaufreland. During a secret meeting with the fashion designer, Vaufreland offered her a deal: become an agent for Berlin, and her nephew would go free and unharmed. That is how Coco Chanel got the code name: Westminster.

Chanel's first assignment was to gather political information in Madrid. She traveled to the city under the guise of having some business to deal with. While there, she met with British Diplomat Brian Wallace. The extent of their conversation is not known, but it is believed they talked about relations between Germany and France. Both allegedly expressed concerns about the rising tensions between the countries.

The information she obtained for her new bosses was enough to impress them. Palasse was released from his prison. But her goals were far from met.

Her business partners, the Wertheimers, transferred their shares of the perfume line to Félix Amiot, a Frenchman. They then fled to the United States for safety.

Double Crossed

With World War II becoming bloodier by the day, Chanel was tasked with a new mission. General Walter Schellenberg wanted his fashionable spy to use her personal relationship with Winston Churchill to bring about the end of the war. At this point, Churchill was Prime Minister of England and was said to be waiting on word that SS Officers were tired of losing their soldiers.

To make their meeting even more special, Chanel arranged for the release of a mutual friend, Vera Lombardi. The women traveled to Madrid with Dincklage. Once they arrived, Lombardi was instructed to hand over a letter Chanel wrote to Churchill.

However, Lombardi was disgusted with the war and particularly with her friend. At the first chance she got, Lombardi decried Chanel as a German spy and made a scene. This did not sit well with the German officers, and they took Lombardi back into custody.

Chanel fled to Paris, where she stayed safe.

End Of Her Spy Career

As French forces reclaimed Paris, Chanel was arrested and questioned about her role as a German spy. Whatever she answered, it was good enough for French authorities to release her. Once freed, she fled to Switzerland.

As the war wound down, there were still questions to be answered. Chanel appeared in a French court again to address her time as a spy. This time, she is on record as saying that she only gave enough information to German forces to save her nephew. She denied any more involvement in the Nazi cause. It was enough to keep her out of trouble.

Chanel made sure to erase any mention and all evidence that she had been a spy for the Nazis. When she learned that Schellenberg was ill, she paid his medical bills and gifted his family with an allowance. His subsequent memoir made no mention of Chanel being one of his agents.

At some point, Chanel made up with the Wertheimer family, and they made a splashy return to the fashion world in 1954. She would remain a top celebrity in the fashion world until her death on January 10, 1971.

It was only in recent years that her time as a spy reemerged as part of her story.

CHAPTER FIVE

Drag Race Scandal Explodes

Willam Belli has company on Ru Paul's banned list. Sherry Pie is joining Belli as only the second person disqualified from Ru Paul's Drag Race in the reality show's 12 season history. Pie, unlike Belli, committed serious crimes and traumatized young men as a result of her shenanigans.

The popular Manhattan drag queen pretended to be a casting agent for a play. Then lured these young men into various states of undress, dangling a part in the production over their heads. At least two of them have admitted to masturbating on camera as part of the audition process.

The drama began unfolding as season 12 of the veteran reality show premiered across multiple networks and across the vast CBSVicaom platform. The show will go on, but Sherry Pie will not film any more episodes because of her actions.

It Started With Facebook

Ben Shimkus started the ball rolling by writing a heartfelt Facebook post. In it, he alleges that Sherry Pie, aka Joey Gugliemelli, tricked him into sending disturbing and embarrassing photos and videos of himself.

It started when he was at Cortland State University. He and Sherry were part of a camp together. A friend offered to put him in contact with a contact, Allison Mossie. This person was said to have been working with Playwrights Horizons in New York City and putting together a play called Bulk. Shimkus alleges that he and "Mossie" exchanged 150 emails. Those missives covered everything one can imagine.

Most of the messages centered around developing the character Jeff. Part of the process had Shimkus filming videos of himself performing scenes from the "still being developed" play, including him sniffing his own armpits. The young actor says, "It was very damaging to me at the time."

One day, Shimkus grew tired of the constant emailing and obvious lies, so he called Playwright Horizons. He was informed that until he called, they had never heard of Allison Mossie before.

Shimkus said: "I don't know who these videos were sent to, and I didn't know what they were objectively for, I felt awful. I felt like I had been completely taken advantage of."

Down Under Actor Grooming
Josh Lillyman says he too was conned by Sherry Pie. Once again, the drag queen used the fictional play Bulk. He was encouraged to share personal stories with "Allison Mossie" just as Shimkus had. Unlike in the Shimkus case, though, Lillyman was encouraged to work with Joey Gugliemelli. The email said the friend was a dynamic performer and often knew what she wanted before she (Mossie) knew what was needed for a scene.

As Lillyman continued to talk with Mossie, he began working with Gugliemenelli to get the perfect audition tape. During the shoot of the scene, Gugliemenelli convinced the young man to take off his shirt and do some flexing. While it seemed strange, Gugliemenelli went along

18

with the suggestion.

Then Gugliemenelli suggested Lillyman go to the bathroom and pleasure himself to feel more macho. After some quick reasoning, the actor decided to do it.

Having had success with getting the young stud to masturbate in the bathroom, Pie then upped the ante and convinced the young man to masturbate on camera. Only the casting director would see the video. Lillyman agreed; he wanted the role more than anything.

Later, while at the bar with friends, Lillyman was stunned to learn a buddy of his was also up for a role in Bulk. His role. Unlike Lillyman and other actors, Landon Summers would not take off his clothes on camera.

Once Joey Gugliemenelli left, and the emails from Allisson Mossie stopped, it came out that the woman never existed. Lillyman said: "I realized I'm an idiot, and I figured it out; it fell apart in less than a day."

Another Bulk Actor
A fifth actor came forward with his own Sherry Pie story. He claims that while he was working with Unified Professional Theatre Auditions, a woman contacted him through his website. This woman referred the actor to Joey Gugliemenelli and told him to call the drag performer. Not needing to be told twice, the actor did.

As was the case with the other actors, this anonymous man was told he was auditioning for a part in a new play called Bulk. He sent over pictures of himself in various states of undress, along with his measurements.

There would be no word if Gugliemenelli tried to get this young man to perform self-love on camera, though it is believed he did. It was his standard MO.

Sherry Pie has tried to leave all of this in the past and sweep it under the rug. In a post on Facebook, the drag queen said that she had no idea how hurtful her actions were. There is also the obligatory apology and hope for moving on. It didn't quite pan out as the older man had hoped it would.

Bye Bye Miss Sherry Pie
VH1 and Viacom wasted no time in addressing the controversy. They released Sherry Pie from her contract, though the show will go on as planned because of the other queens. It would not be fair to take away their chance at stardom because of one bad queen. Here's what the production company said:

"In light of recent developments and Sherry Pie's statement, Sherry Pie has been disqualified from RuPaul's Drag Race; out of respect for the hard work of the other queens, VH1 will air the season as planned. Sherry will not appear in the grand finale scheduled to be filmed later this spring."

When they disqualified Willam Belli, they went through the motions of having a "lip sync for your life" segment with Sharon Needles and Phi Phi O'Hara. Once it was over, Belli was called back to the stage and released from his contract. It could be the same situation with Sherry Pie. Though, there is no word on how far Pie got into the season.

There could be criminal charges against Gugliemenelli as well. Depending on how the actors who submitted the photos and videos to him react, there could be fraud and/or revenge porn charges brought against him.

Ed Anderson

CHAPTER SIX

Man Tried To Steal Halle Berry's House

Real estate is torturous. Sometimes you find a house you want, one that would make all of your dreams come true. Then in a cruel fashion, the universe will take it away from you. All because it already has another owner. Like if you were a cool house, you would not already have an owner. Just saying.

Ronald Eugene Griffin appeared to take the saying "desperate times call for desperate measures" a little too far. His nefarious plan started in January. He showed up at Berry's residence and jiggled the locks. Berry's gardener scared him off. But like an obsessed lover, Griffin would not leave well enough be.

Return of The Griffin

In March, Griffin returned to the house. Halle Berry was nowhere near the property, and it is believed that Griffin just really loved the house and was not trying to get close to the Oscar Winner.

Once again, the gardener tried to scare the man off, but this time was not successful. Griffin called the cops on the gardener and claimed he was trespassing on his property. The cops looked at the documents he gave them. Right away, they knew he had forged the documents. What good is the internet for if you can't fake documents or hire a hitman successfully?

If it weren't for Facebook and celebs acting naughty....

House Arrest

On June 20, 2019, Police apprehended Griffin without incident. He is being charged with procuring and offering a false warranty deed and petty theft. Police said in a statement: "Griffin had changed the title of the residence without the victim's knowledge and attempted to forcibly gain entry onto the house."

They continued on to say: "Upon arrival, officers were met by employees of the residence, who knew the true property owner of the residence. They reported that suspect Ronald Eugene Griffin was trying to gain entry by compromising the locks of the residence. Suspect Griffin claimed to be the new owner of the residence." And he would've gotten away with it too if it weren't a stupid plan.

Also, petty theft? Berry's house is worth an estimated $3.8 million. How is that petty theft? That sounds more like grand larceny.

CHAPTER SEVEN

Disappearance Of A Basketball Star

Rico Harris always made an impression. Many were impressed by his athletic ability; he was recruited by the NBA after he graduated high school. Harris also stood out by his height. At 6'9", Rico towered over most people. He was also known as one of the kindest people around.

The gentle giant also had some big issues, though. One of those issues was an addiction problem that would taint most of his adult life.

However, things seemed to be coming together for Harris. Before he disappeared.

College Addiction
Harris was sought after by many colleges for their basketball teams when he graduated high school in the 1990s. The NBA reportedly sent him messages about skipping university to join a team. As he pondered his choices, he realized how lucky he was.

It was likely that he would be able to keep a promise to his mother. He had long sworn he would support his mother.

Even with that promise in mind, he chose to go to school in Arizona. Many say this choice signaled the beginning of a severe problem for

Harris.

He and some teammates faced some disciplinary action at the school for false imprisonment. Nothing happened to them. But Harris would soon leave the school because he was drinking a lot. Therefore, he was unable to pass classes.

After he left Arizona State, he joined the basketball team at Los Angeles City College (LACC). This was not a good choice. His addiction went from bad to worse. Harris was drinking a lot. After an undisclosed incident with a student, he was given a six-game suspension for being intoxicated.

He left the school shortly after that.

Globetrotting And Rehab
After leaving LACC, he joined the Harlem Globetrotters. It was a professional high. Many believed it was the beginning of something special for Harris. But after just a few months on the job, he quit.

There were some loved ones who blamed his alcoholism. While others say that he was nursing an injury from breaking up a bar fight. In either case, his leaving exasperated the substance abuse problem,

It brought the addiction to a head.

Eventually, Harris was convinced to go to rehab. He did and got clean. After leaving the clinic, he worked as a cook for The Salvation Army. He did a good job, and that led to him being hired as a security guard.

Love And Disappearing

While working as a security guard for an event, he met his girlfriend, Jennifer Song. In a meet-cute moment worthy of a rom-com movie, Rico snapped Jennifer's picture and asked if he could text it to her — their bond grew from that moment.

Their relationship moved swiftly, and soon they agreed to move in together. The caveat was Harris would be relocating to Seattle to be with her. He moved his belongings up to the new house.

Then he went back to LA to say goodbye to his mom. Stories begin to diverge significantly during this time. Harris's mom claims that she encouraged him to stay the night at her house since he had been awake for more than 30 hours.

Friends discount that version of events. They claim Harris and his mom had an argument, and he was forced to leave the house.

In either case, it was the last time that Rico was ever seen alive.

Disappearance Mystery Deepens

On October 13, 2014, a Yolo County Cop saw an abandoned black Nissan in a parking lot. He made a note of it and ran the plates. The car belonged to Harris, but he was nowhere to be found.

The next day, the cop came back, and the car was there. Since the car appeared to be abandoned, the officer called to have it towed. When the tow truck arrived, they discovered the car battery was dead.

A family found a cell phone and leather bag filled with clothes in the nearby woods. They searched the bag to see who it belonged to. There was no wallet or identification inside the bag. And the phone was dead. The family turned it over to the police.

The cops charged the phone and watched the last video that was taken.

Harris was seen rifling through papers in the glove compartment and muttering swears in the video. There was no indication as to what he was looking for.

The only other clues as to his whereabouts were some footprints going into the woods. This lead police to believe that Harris had simply decided to disappear and start a new life.

Theories Debunked

It is a foolish theory since someone of Harris's stature and even fame level would not go unrecognized for very long. Even if he was considered a D-list celebrity, there would be fans who recognized him. And his height would make him stand out in every crowd. Literally.

There are some theories that Harris may have committed suicide. These theories cannot be as easily dismissed as he quietly went about living undetected. He had recently relapsed. But the future seemed bright for him and Jennifer Song. They had discussed their future, including marriage and having babies. The biggest problem with this theory is that his body was not found. Someone would have come along and found the body by now if he committed suicide.

Another theory suggests that Harris was pulled over, and things escalated. He disappeared just after the Ferguson, Missouri police killed Michael Brown. Police brutality was being highlighted often on the news. If he was pulled over, Harris filming his interaction with the cop would make sense. It also explains why he was looking in his glove box for papers. The cop could have grown agitated and ordered the giant out of the car. If Harris had been drinking, maybe he ran. The cop could have shot him in the woods and realized what he had done. A coverup would not be hard to pull off in this case.

The truth about what happened to Rico Harris may never be known. If it is a coverup, there is no way for the police department to come forward and tell the truth now. Especially since they put forth such a foolish and easily disproven theory out.

CHAPTER EIGHT

Cheating Football Player Caught By Wife

Being in the public eye amplifies things. Celebrities often will complain about the spotlight, even as they seek it out. This is especially true when their relationship hits a rough patch, or there is a breakup.

To compound the hypocrisy, some celebrities will utilize their publicity teams in an effort to make their former partner look bad. They slip stories of infidelity to the tabloids. This, despite the amicable split story, they spin to the mainstream media.

Earl and Nina Thomas seem to be taking a page from that playbook with their latest situation. It includes a confrontation with a gun and Nina facing some serious charges.

The Argument That Started It All

Earl Thomas is a safety for the Baltimore Ravens. He married his wife, Nina, on April 16, 2016. The wedding was extravagant and star-studded. They seemed to be a happy couple, with very few rumors about infidelity surrounding them. It seemed like a fairy tale.

But not every fairy tale has a happy ending.

Just three days before their anniversary, Earl and Nina got into an

29

argument. Reports suggest that Nina was tired of Earl's drinking. It got out of control. Earl called his brother, Seth Thomas, and asked Seth to pick him up.

He did—much to Nina's dismay.

Social Gun

As the hours stretched on, Nina felt her fury building. Then she looked at Earl's Snapchat and saw him in a video with another woman. It was the final straw for her. She called up a couple of friends and asked them to come with her to confront her cheating husband and the other female.

Using Earl's location on Snapchat, Nina was able to track him to a nearby house that served as an Airbnb. Once her girls showed up, Nina grabbed Earl's 9mm Berretta. She told police she took the gun to "scare him."

When the three women entered the Airbnb, they found Earl and Seth naked in bed with other women. Irate, Nina held the gun to her husband's head. Screaming at him.

She claims there was no intention of hurting him. Nina told police"that she took out the magazine thinking that the gun could not fire." What she didn't know was that there was still a bullet in the chamber.

A struggle ensued as Earl tried to wrest the gun out of his wife's hands. Reportedly she hit him several times during their fight over the weapon. After he got the gun from her, Nina got a knife and started chasing him around with it.

As she chased her husband, Nina reportedly screamed at her

husband's lover: "I got something for all you hoes!"

Caught On Camera
One of the women took out her phone and recorded the entire incident. When police watched it, they noted that Nina held the gun less than a foot away from Earl's head. It was also noted that, as Earl stated, she did hit him quite a few times.

According to the police report, they responded to a domestic disturbance call around 3:41 am.

They also say: "we observed that a black female wearing an orange sweater with a knife in her hand, later identified as Nina Thomas, was chasing a shirtless black male, later identified as Earl Thomas, with a pistol in his hand around a vehicle."

After interviewing everyone involved, Nina was arrested. She is being charged with burglary of a residence with the intent to commit aggravated assault with a deadly weapon and family violence. She is currently out on bond.

Earl and the woman he was with both have a personal protection order against Nina. It requires her to stay at least 200 yards away from them.

Nina believes that she was "wrongfully arrested," according to a statement from her attorney. She plans on fighting the charges in court.

The Baltimore Ravens were not notified of the incident and had no comment. Not surprising since Earl was not arrested.

Earl released a statement on social media: "Instead of talking about us, just keep us in y'all prayers; stuff like this happens. We try to live the best lives we possibly can. Sometimes it doesn't go as planned."

CHAPTER NINE

Sex Tapes Dumped In Ocean To Avoid Scandal

There was never any doubt that the "King of Porn" had sex tapes and naked pictures of celebs; that was almost a given. The real question was what would he do with them, or what would happen when he was no longer among the living. It has been revealed that Hugh Hefner had already thought about this and decided that his secrets would follow him to the grave, or at least as many of them as he could possibly take with him.

One day as his health was deteriorating, Hef thought to himself that he should do something about the stash of porn that he had hidden away from the world. Not like a teenage boy hiding his Playboys from his parents, more like a murderer hiding evidence from the police. If the evidence was naked pictures and videotaped proof of Hef having sex with women and the police were the paparazzi and gossipmongers. But what to do with it?

Why not throw it into the bottom of the Pacific Ocean? Not something that most people would do but then how many of us can claim to have had sex with more women than have appeared in the pages of his infamous magazine. A source revealed, "Hugh was terrified of the world finding out everything about his past," a source revealed. "He had kept a treasure chest of memories of his life with all these beautiful women dating back from the 1950s to the mid-1990s." It seems counterintuitive that he felt this way because, well, he founded Playboy and threw lavish parties that usually ended up in orgies.

Swinging Both Ways

There was more than that, though; some celebrity men were among the pictures and videos. It's unclear if they were having sex with Hef, but rumor has always been that he swung both ways. The source said, "Some famous male movie stars too were in those videos and had that come out, it would have been a huge scandal." Why would it have been a scandal if the men were not engaged in sexual relations with the Bunny master? Maybe someone should do a deep dive into the Pacific Ocean to find these treasures, see if they can be preserved. Probably not, but it would be worth a try.

The real reason he wanted this treasure trove of porn destroyed is very altruistic. Hef was afraid of what would happen if these saw the light of day, the lives it would ruin, so he decided to destroy the stash instead. "Hugh explained that he didn't want anyone's lives, marriages, or careers to be destroyed by what he had In his library. Joe did it and never told anyone." The Joe mentioned in the quote is Joe Piastro, who was the head of security for Hefner. Piastro died in 2011. What made Hugh Hefner worry about the tapes being stolen and released in the first place?

The 90s Connection

Two words: Pamela Anderson. For those that don't remember in the 1990s, Anderson had two sex tapes stolen, one with ex-husband Tommy Lee and Brett Michaels. Lee became more known for the size of his cock than his music, especially to a younger generation. Those stolen tapes made him "so upset and paranoid that he decided it was best to have them disappear. He didn't trust people to burn them in case they got stolen, so he charged Joe with getting rid of them in the ocean." When that was done, he must have felt better.

There it is. The man who brought pornography into the mainstream was so worried about his own sexual escapades being exploited that he had thousands of pictures and tape destroyed. Were they for public consumption? No. However, then it could be argued that the women's bodies that appeared in Playboy magazine over the years were not either. Now to go to the Pacific Ocean, for something else.

CHAPTER TEN

Socially Gruesome Murder Of An Egirl

There are people who crave attention and will do anything to get it. Bianca Devins was not that type of person, though she was a popular personality on social media outlets like Discord, Instagram, and 4Chan. It was on Discord that she met a person who was an attention seeker, someone who would do anything to be adored by the public.

That man would be Brandon Andrew Clark. He met Devins via a gamer messaging social media outlet, Discord. Clark appeared to have romantic feelings for her. As their conversation progressed, he took his shot and asked her on a date. It seemed to be spontaneous, but it was not.

He had everything planned.

Everything.

Socially Active
Bianca Devins was a popular social media figure. She would post pictures for straight males, who nobody wanted to have sex with, to enjoy. And they did. Because of the images, she was one of the most famous figures on the Discord. On Instagram, she also saw her popularity soar.

Many young men would slide into Devins' DMs. It is believed she responded to nearly all of the messages that were sent to her. There were a lot of flirty conversations and allegedly some naked pictures being sent back and forth. Some of the males seemed to be quite taken with the burgeoning social media star.

One of the enamored men that Devins was talking to happened to be Brandon Andrew Clark. Their conversation started out friendly, if not a bit flirty. He began to express a romantic interest in her, but she declined the advances at first. Eventually, he asked her on a date. He bought tickets to a concert in New York City, she agreed to go.

This would prove to be a fatal mistake.

Green With Murder

Clark bought tickets for the two of them to go see Nicole Dollanger in concert. The event was in Queens, New York, which required them to drive from Utica to the show. Devins believed they were going to the singer live as friends, but her escort thought otherwise.

Leading up to the concert, he had been pushing Devins to be in a monogamous relationship. Each time Clark brought it up, she would decline. Something that bothered him greatly. He believed the concert would be a turning point in their relationship, that she would be obligated to be his girl.

At the concert, Devins found a guy she liked and was making out with him. Clark was disgruntled by this. He was embarrassed and felt disrespected since the woman he loved was kissing another man. It was not something that he was going to let go of.

On the drive home, Devins fell asleep. Clark was seething and woke her up. He let her know he felt it was inappropriate for her to be messing around with another man. She countered that they weren't a couple, and furthermore, she had no interest in being monogamous with him.

Hearing the words triggered Clark once again. But this time, he had a plan to deal with the situation.

Kill And Share

After Devins denies his request to be with him, Clark hits her. Repeatedly. When he goes to strike her again, Devins threatens to get out of the car and walk the rest of the way home. This sets Clark off, and he grabs a knife that he brought with him. He thrusts it into her several times, ending her life.

Mr. Clark recorded the entire exchange on his phone, which had been placed on the dashboard. After Devins was dead, he took pictures of her body and posted them to Instagram and Discord. It was his way of letting everyone know that she was gone. He proceeded to attempt to take his own life.

Police showed up just before his attempt was successful because the images of Devins' death were widely shared on both social media platforms. One viewer tipped them off. They also found the video footage of the murder.

It was a slam dunk case for them.

Defending The Indefensible

Members of the social media platform, 4chan, cheered Devins' death. They left messages in support of Clark, saying that she deserved it. Some of the letters went as far as to say that Devins should not have turned down their "bro," and because she did, her death was the work of God. 4Chan left the messages up.

Facebook, Instagram, and Discord all took the posts revolving around Devins' death down. They banned hashtags like #YesJuliet. Clark's profiles were taken down and banned. And the Discord server that shared the photos of Devins' corpse was terminated and prohibited from being brought back.

In relation to the social media blackout, Clark initially told the police that he blacked out and did not remember committing the murder. They believe he was attempting to set up a temporary insanity defense.

In February 2020, Clark changed his plea from not guilty to guilty. He faces 25 years to life in prison when he is sentenced.

CHAPTER ELEVEN

Tragic Life Of A Funny Man

Phil Hartman. It's a name that brings back warm feelings, maybe even a few chuckles. That's because he was a legendary comedian, known for his raucous humor that was designed to make a point but clean enough for the whole family.

Hartman was best known for his stints on Saturday Night Live, The Simpsons, and his star vehicle, NewsRadio. Fans flocked to each show and watched as their favorite was able to milk laughs from even the most minute lines.

He seemed to be on top of the world. But underneath the surface lie emotional problems that followed him throughout his life.

The Past Is Never Far Away
In the early '70s, Hartman grew facial hair and subscriber to the hippie doctrine. He was all about free love and a gypsy lifestyle on the road. As a result, he worked as a roadie for Rockin Foo. His duties included designing their album covers, something he was quite astute at.

While working with the band, he met his first wife, Gretchen Lewis. They were hot and heavy for a while, unable to keep their hands off of one another. They married in 1970, but the chemistry and relationship came to a crashing halt in 1972. The once fairy tale marriage ended in a bitter divorce.

Hartman was feeling restless around that time and left his roadie job. While living his bohemian lifestyle, the comedian found two things he would come to love a lot. One of those things was guns. He bought quite a few of them and became an enthusiast. Dawna Kaufmann was the other thing he found.

Kaufmann was a comedy writer who thought that her new beau was very funny. She encouraged him to join The Groundlings. When he told her about his gun collection, she didn't believe him. Her jaw dropped when he showed it to her.

Comedy Is The Sound Of Love

The Groundlings welcomed Hartman to their ranks in 1975. Audiences loved him and his flair for witty comedy. His characters grew in popularity, and his stature within the group grew.

As did his reputation for being a flirt with the ladies. This did not sit well with Kaufmann and led to many fights between them. After many years together, they ended up breaking up. Even though their relationship came to an end, the pair remained close friends.

After the breakup, Hartman met Brynn Omdahl. She took his breath away. As with Lewis, the chemistry between the popular comic and his new gal pal was off the charts. But everything was not as perfect as they wanted friends and family to think it was.

Omdahl was an addict. Hartman encouraged his lady love to go to rehab and get the help that she needed. That suggestion led to many heated arguments between the pair.

Despite the conflict, Hartman and Omdahl got married.

Saturday Night Fight

In 1986, Hartman joined the cast of Saturday Night Live. According to Lorne Michaels, Hartman "has done more work that's touched greatness than probably anybody else who's ever been here."

He was a popular addition to the cast. The audience loved him, as did his costars. They have credited him with helping them be better in sketches and working to make sure the sketches that made it to air were the best they could be.

One of those costars was Jan Hooks. She was his most frequent scene partner. Hooks said she had a "deep, platonic love for him." Even though they were only friends, he would say crass and dirty things to her. Things that would not hold up well in the #MeToo era. One joke she shared was after a skit that had them making out, he whispered to her: "You gave me a huge boner. Oh god, I've got to run."

Hartman mentored Chris Farrelly. The actors got along fine on and offscreen, according to those who knew that. However, he did not appreciate the direction the show was taking. He felt it was sophomoric. He began to think about leaving the show.

Not Done Yet

There was a contract to honor, though. Even with his unease at the direction of the show, Hartman was a consummate professional and honored the commitment he made.

With the rise in popularity of Dana Carvey and Jon Lovitz, he grew even more disenfranchised with the show. But he was able to go work on other shows like The Simpsons. His voice performance proved to be very popular on the animated sitcom and with the production staff of the show. A one-time guest appearance turned into a recurring gig.

While Hartman was enjoying the success that came with his hard work, his wife was in a tailspin. As the fan mail piled up for him, she grew resentful. Eventually, she fell off the wagon. Omdahl started abusing drugs and alcohol on a regular basis. It led to many fights between the couple.

Omdahl worried about their marriage imploding, citing Hartman's past relationships as the reason for her concern. While he never cheated on her, it was not for lack of opportunity. Something that bothered his wife and fueled her desire to numb herself from reality.

One drunken incident happened in the SNL writers' room. Omdahl came in while they were busy putting together a show. She sat on another man's lap and stuck her tongue in his ear. While Hartman did not appear to be angry about it, several people in the room said he ushered her out of the building with the threat of divorce.

Shortly after that, Hartman's contract was up. He decided to exit.

Success And Stress
After leaving SNL, Hartman landed a new sitcom, NewsRadio. Once again, he was a hit with his castmates. While the show was never a breakout hit, it had a solid following, and the critics loved it.

Omdahl's irrational and destructive behavior continued. With that, Hartman was pushed closer to his costar, Vicki Lewis. She was dealing with her own relationship issues. Her boyfriend, actor Nick Nolte, was also an addict. The similarity in their situations allowed them to bond.

Hartman's fame was a double-edged sword. It gave them financial security but intensified Omdahl's insecurities. Things began to go south on the homefront.

With the drug use increasing and the fighting becoming a daily occurrence, Hartman began to think about divorcing his wife. He was tired of her tantrums and her throwing vases in an attempt to get what she wanted.

As a last-ditch effort to save their union, they went to marriage counseling. Hartman admitted that he was no longer attracted to his wife because of her issues, and he had no interest in having sex with her. Her addiction had become too much for him to bear.

Omdahl was angry when she learned that her husband promised his mother that he would file for divorce the next time she came home drunk and/or high. He also planned to take the kids with him.

Save The Marriage, Lose Life
Omdahl tried to find a way to save the marriage. After explaining to the doctor about what was happening, the doctor prescribed Zoloft. However, instead of helping to stabilize her mood, she became even more irrational and violent.

The reason Zoloft didn't work to help stabilize her mood is that Omdahl continued to consume alcohol while on it. The effects of drinking and taking Zoloft are an inability to sleep and confused brain chemicals.

On May 27, 1998, with the marriage falling completely apart and Omdahl feeling as if she was losing control, she went to a friend's and had drinks. She lamented the state of her marriage and complained about the impending divorce. After having a few drinks, she left to go see another friend's house.

Ron Douglas told police that Omdahl had more drinks with him. She also continued to complain about Hartman wanting to leave her. They shared a few drinks, and she seemed to settle down.

Then she went home.

Murder And Suicide In One Night

Once Omdahl got home, she and Hartman got into a huge fight about her drinking. He began to pack up his clothes as their argument spiraled out of control. She warned him if he tried to leave, she would murder him.

Hartman didn't care at this point. He was over the marriage, over the constant fighting. Rumors have surfaced that he had another lady love that he planned on moving in with after his divorce was finalized. The other woman is said to have been Vicki Lewis.

However, that was not meant to be. After taking a break for a moment and laying in the bed he shared with his wife, she joined him. Omdahl had grabbed his Smith & Wesson .38, she pointed it at him. With less than a foot between them, she pulled the trigger and killed her husband.

Omdahl went back over to Douglas' house. She was even drunker and clearly unstable. She told him what happened, but he thought it was hyperbole. He went back to the Hartman's house with her and discovered that she was being honest about what happened.

He called the police.

As her friend called the police, Omdahl called her sister. She requested theater love be sent to the kids and that she regretted what she had done.

Then she laid in the bed with her husband and pulled the trigger for a second time that night. Ending her own life.

The death of Phil Hartman and his wife broke shortly after. Magazines covered it as a tragedy. Many have used Omdahl's breakdown as a call to get funding for mental illness and addiction centers.

CHAPTER TWELVE

Star Steals Movie Props From Set

Some things are just too good to be true. This was my thought as I recorded an episode of Drunk Gossip, my podcast. There was a missing segment that needed to be filled, and then my celebrity gossip alert sounded off — the snippet read "Sean Young wanted by the police." Celebrity gossip and true crime? It was a win/win! Why is the actress wanted? She was caught on tape stealing production computers from Charley Boy, a film she was supposed to direct.

To understand what happened, let's back up a bit. Charlie Boy was filmed in Astoria, Brooklyn. What is it about Brooklyn that these bizarre crimes keep happening? Thomas Hines was brought in to help get the film going because there had been clashes between Young and the cast. Hines says, "I think that she was in over her head, and I realized... I was making choices that were actually going to allow this movie to get made, which it did." But things were not going as well as Hines had hoped they were. Young tried to fire him. The Executive Producers then decided that she was the problem and fired her instead.

Damage And Theft

Apparently, she took this to mean that she should cause some real damage since she was the problem. Young went back to get some personal items and began taking out things that belonged to the production company. The staff changed the locks because something seemed amiss. Hines reveals, "We were concerned because we all got the feeling that she didn't want to come in here just to pick up her stuff, and that's why she kept leaving things here." Why did it take them so long to figure out that something was wrong? And how did Sean Young figure out a way around this?

How did she get to the computers? The production and police believe that she recruited her son, Quinn, to help. Since the doors were locked, film employees' chances of letting her into the offices were very slim. So they improvised. They went through the bathroom window! Yes, really! And they did this in front of cameras! That cannot be stressed enough. "You can see her stealing the computer equipment and going and coming and going as if it was 1945, and there aren't cameras everywhere on 4K," Hines explains. For those that aren't sure or don't know, 4K cameras are a very high resolution. Young and her son were caught stealing red-handed. There is no plausible explanation for this. Hines finished, "There is a warrant out for her arrest right now, and she is going to be arrested, And she is going to jail for this because basically, this is the stupidest thing she has ever done in her life." Hold my beer, classic Sean Young says.

History Of Histrionics
This is not the first time that Young has acted irrationally on a movie set. In 1989, the actress was cast as Catwoman in Tim Burton's Batman. Alas, she injured her arm, and with that, the role ultimately went to Kim Bassinger. That did not deter Young. She fashioned her own Catwoman costume and accosted Tim Burton and Batman himself, Michael Keaton. When they didn't budge or fire Bassinger, Young took her act to The Joan Rivers Show. For many years, Sean Young was blacklisted because of that stunt. This may do the same thing to an already fragile career.

This would be funny if it weren't so tragic. At one time, Young was a rising star. She had her pick of roles. Now she'll be lucky if she gets to pick which bunk bed she sleeps on in jail. Some things are too sad to be true.

CHAPTER THIRTEEN

Old Hollywood's Most Scandalous Romance

In the studio system days of Hollywood, actors and actresses had very little say in the movies they made or the relationships the public saw them in. Studio heads felt entitled to control every aspect of the celebrities' lives since they invested money in creating the audiences' images.

One of the most notorious studio moguls was Harry Cohn, who ran Columbia Pictures. Instead of growing a stable of stars like other production companies were known to do, Cohn would poach his contract players from his competitors. He would pair them with supporting actors that he was grooming to be top actors.

Rita Hayworth was one of the actresses that had been groomed by Cohn. While the studio head had expected absolute loyalty from his ingenue, Hayworth lived by her own rules. The much-married starlet saw her box office receipts drop every time she found a new husband, much to Cohn's dismay. Since he felt that Hayworth was not showing enough gratitude to him, he decided to bring another female star.

Kim Novak was the actress he decided to turn into his next star. Cohn spent a lot of time making sure he got his revenge on Hayworth for her perceived misbehavior. The studio head took great pains to make sure his newest starlet would stay in line and follow his instructions to a "T."

And she would, until a fateful night in 1957. That was the night she fell in love.

Crooning A New Tune

Sammy Davis Jr. was performing at Chez Paree. By this point in his career, he was known as the world's greatest performer. There was electricity in the air as he took the stage. Cheers from the audience fed the talented singer's energy.

Kim Novak was in the audience. Her gaze was fixed on Davis Jr. The crooner took notice and began to sing directly to her. After the first set, the other people in attendance were buzzing about the sparks between the two stars. The rumor mill kicked into high gear when they began to ask friends about one another.

For Novak, the night out was a reward after a challenging shoot on Alfred Hitchcock's Vertigo. Davis Jr. was enjoying his ascension on the celebrity ladder. Tony Curtis and Janet Leigh decided to play matchmaker and invite the two to a soiree.

After the party, word began to spread about Novak and Davis Jr. being an item. The story appeared as a blind item in a gossip column.

Fans of both were shocked and dismayed. An interracial romance between the two stars threatened to end both of their careers. And could have landed them in jail in most states.

When Davis Jr. saw the item, he called Noval and apologized to her. True to her rebellious nature, the movie star assured him that the studio didn't own her and she cared deeply about him. At the end of their phone call, Novak invited the singer over for a spaghetti dinner.

An Affair To Continue

Throughout 1957, Novak and Davis Jr. defied public opinion. They continued to date. Arthur Silber, a friend of Davis Jr.'s, would chauffeur the couple to a Malibu beach house.

Davis also had a private line put into his hotel room in Vegas, so his employers wouldn't listen in on their calls. Despite or maybe because of the subterfuge, the love between the two grew.

When Novak returned to Chicago for the holidays in December 1957. Davis Jr. missed his lady love so much that he found someone to take over his show for him. He then flew out to spend Christmas with her.

Rumors that the pair were going to get married hit a fever pitch. Gossip columns were filled with stories about the couple tying the knot. Some even reported that Davis Jr. and Novak had requested a marriage license.

Hollywood and the world were torn about the possible union. It didn't deter the couple. They basked in their love.

For as long as they could.

The Breakup Plot

When Cohn heard that Novak planned on marrying David Jr., he had a heart attack. As he recovered, he plotted ways to break the couple up. The studio head would rant to anyone that would listen that Novak was his property. Her betrayal would not go unpunished.

To break the couple up, Cohn called mobster John Roselli. They devised a plan to kidnap Davis Jr. and force him to break up with

Novak. The crooner was warned that the interracial relationship would harm the movie studio while being held by the mob. If that were to happen, things would turn nasty for him.

Novak and Davis Jr. resisted ending their relationship, Cohn took things to an extreme. He placed a hit on the singer. A clock was ticking, and the only way it would stop is if they broke up.

Davis Jr. asked his friend, Chicago mobster Sam Giancana, for help. Alas, the only protection that could be offered was for Chicago and Las Vegas. Giancana had no reach in Hollywood.

The breakup of Davis Jr. and Novak made headlines in Hollywood. Gossip columnists fought for exclusives on what really went down. The Confidential magazine began asking friends and coworkers of the pair what they knew.

One source told them that Davis Jr. had been threatened. The singer was ordered to forget about Novak and marry a black woman. Something he did days after the breakup became public knowledge.

After The Relationship
Davis Jr. married his ex-girlfriend, Loray White. He paid her to be his wife for less than a year. The goal was to keep him safe from the mob while the heat from his relationship with Novak cooled off.

The stress of being married to White and missing Novak depressed the singer. He was found pointing a gun to his head. When his friend asked him why he wanted to end his life, Davis Jr. asked why he wasn't allowed to just live his life the way he wanted to.

Novak was concerned about her former lover but kept her distance. She would start to get her revenge on Cohn. When she was loaned out to other studios, the studio head would be paid a lot of money. She was only given a fraction of the payment.

She took to the press and complained about it. Cohn was furious as public sentiment turned against him, and Novak was held in high esteem. In the 1960s, she left Hollywood and moved to Big Sur. The movie star took up painting and raising horses to fill her time. Through the 70s and 80s, she would make the occasional film appearance, but acting was no longer her focus. In 1992, she retired from acting altogether.

Novak and Davis Jr. would be reunited for the 1979 Academy Awards. They were seen dancing together. They would meet just one more time: As Sammy Davis Jr. lay in the hospital dying. The meeting was said to have lifted his spirits in the final hours of his life.

A forbidden love exposed the seedier side of Hollywood. Racism and prejudice destroyed two people's lives.

CHAPTER FOURTEEN

Crimes Of A Passionate Fan

Superfans, also known as stans, come along with the package of being a celebrity. They are so pervasive that Eminem wrote a whole song about them. In his piece, an unhinged man writes letters to the rapper with increasing intensity. Near the climax of the song, the stan kills his girlfriend and himself, blaming the Grammy winner.

Many roll their eyes at the song. They sing along to it, but they do not believe a person can be that unhinged. It seems impossible that someone could be so obsessed with a celebrity that the fan would commit crimes.

In most cases, the stans are harmless. This group may launch campaigns in the star's name, but for the most part, it ends there.

However, there is a subset of stans who take things too far. It is this group that Eminem was referring to in his song. And it is they who make the news and change the lives of their beloved star forever.

Sometimes even ending the life of the celebrity.

Singer At Heart
Selena Quintanilla started singing at a young age. Her father,

Abraham Quintanilla Jr., noted that she had the voice of an angel. He decided that if she loved music as much as she said she did, they could make some extra money by having a family band. It turned out to be a great decision. The band booked events almost every day of the week.

This ruffled the feathers of Selena's teacher because it interfered with her schooling. One threatened to tell the Texas Board of Education about the young woman's musical career and how her father took her out of school. In response, Abraham said to her that it was none of her business.

Between school and her singing career, Selena was a tired girl. But she pushed through and graduated from the American School of Correspondence in Chicago. She planned on going to college and majoring in business administration. However, her father had other ideas.

Abraham bought an old bus. The family hit the road on tour; the hope was to promote Selena's burgeoning music career. They would book gigs that barely paid enough for the family to eat and buy gasoline for the next job.

That changed in 1984 when Selena signed a record deal with Freddie Records. Her wish was to record songs in English. However, the producers she worked with had other ideas. They led her to record Tejano songs. It was a gambit that paid off.

Selena was a hit.

Promoting Fan

As Selena was promoting the new album, she appeared on The Johnny Canales Show. While appearing on the show, she came to the attention of Rick Trevino, a music manager. He took over the duties of booking gigs but ran into resistance. Tejano music was dominated by men, and owners of clubs were not willing to lose the more popular male stars by booking a woman.

This did not slow Selena's rise. Her albums would go platinum, which thrilled the record executives. The money was rolling in, and the Quintanilla family had enough to feel comfortable.

Other record companies began to take note of Selena. Capitol Records and Sony Music Latin both offered her a record contract. Abraham, who had taken management back, decided to sign with Capitol. He thought they would have a chance at a crossover album, a belief that would prove to be false.

Chris Perez joined the band backing Selena up. He had feelings for the songstress. They would eventually confess their mutual affection for one another at a Pizza Hut.

Perez wasn't the only new addition. In 1991, Yolonda Saldivar asked Abraham if she could launch a fan club in Selena's name. He acquiesced, believing an organization like that would fuel album and concert sales.

Saldivar integrated herself into the family. She grew close to Selena, whom she idolized. Her job as a nurse became burdensome, so she asked permission to run the fan club full time and collect a salary. Once again, Abraham agreed.

The former nurse was about to become a massive part of the Quintanilla family.

Deceitful Ways
With her popularity rising, and cash flowing in, Selena decided to branch out. She opened two boutiques called Selena Etc. The clothes

were designed by Selena's friend, Martin Gomez, with input from the singer herself.

The stores were successful.

Between recording music, touring, and designing clothes, Selena found herself overwhelmed with work. Something needed to be delegated. She talked it over with Perez and her father, it was decided that Saldivar would manage the boutiques for her, in addition to running the fan club.

Gomez didn't like his new officemate. There was something about her that made his skin crawl. He noted that she was oddly possessive of their mutual friend.

The newly appointed boutique manager would make things up. Gomez complained about the hostile work environment to Selena, hoping to oust Saldivar.

The designer left for fashion week in New York. Selena talked to Saldivar about making things tenable at the stores, just keep the peace. On the outside, the former nurse seemed to agree. But she was seething and destroyed clothes that Gomez had been working on before his departure.

He complained once again. This time his complaint got lost in a pile of customer issues. Orders were not being fulfilled, but the money was being taken from their credit cards. Selena and Abraham tried to get to the bottom of the situation. There was just one answer, and nobody liked it.

Saldivar was embezzling the money.

Obsessed To Death

Saldivar admitted to a reporter that she was obsessed with Selena. This put the singer's loved ones even more on edge. They continued to investigate the missing money and unfilled orders.

Abraham began asking the former nurse for missing financial paperwork. She argued with him at first, painting him as a stage dad. The two faced off time after time. Finally, he told her that if she didn't produce the paperwork, he would be forced to go to the police with the matter.

He advised his daughter to steer clear of Saldivar. However, Selena was still unsure that her friend would betray her in such a way. Perez coaxed his wife into seeing things her father's way. There was always the matter of the bank records and other financial papers that Saldivar had held on to.

When they asked about them, the former nurse said she had been sexually assaulted and robbed in Mexico. She needed time to get her strength back. It was only after Selena agreed to go to the doctor with her that Saldivar said she would hand over the pertinent paperwork.

On March 31, 1995, Selena took her friend to the medical clinic. However, Saldivar left after being told she would need to get a rape kit done. They went to the Days Inn, where the former nurse was going to give the financial records to Selena.

After going to the room where Saldivar was staying, she pulled a gun. A confrontation ensued, and Selena was shot in the shoulder. The bullet ripped open the main artery.

She made it to the lobby and identified Saldivar as her killer. Selena died on the way to the hospital.

Trial Moved

Saldivar confessed to the shooting. She said that during a confrontation with Selena, she had threatened to commit suicide. The songstress begged her not to and went to leave. When ordered to close the door, the Grammy-winner did, and the gun went off.

Prosecutors used the confession as the backbone of their case. Defense attorneys argued the cops got the signed admission by coercion and it should not be admitted into evidence. They lost that motion.

However, the judge agreed to move the trial from Selena's hometown to Houston.

After the case was given to the jurors, it took them three hours to deliberate. They returned a conviction. Saldivar was given life in prison.

This was a case of a stan that took things too far.

CHAPTER FIFTEEN

Disappearance Of A Cool Cat By A Kitten

Carole Baskin is known as the cat lady. Her advocacy work for big cats had already earned her a following within the animal rights community. Those who knew her had opinions formed about who she was and the lengths she would go to achieve her goals.

When she began feuding with Joe Maldonado-Passage (aka Joe Exotic), those who knew them sat back and watched the fireworks. Both were passionate about tigers and other felines. Each had their own set of goals, and neither would back down from a fight. The very public feud would make riveting TV.

In fact, it did make for a good TV show. When Netflix debuted Tiger King, most of the comments centered on the rivalry between Baskin and Exotic. There was one part that united everyone from near and far.

Maldonado-Passage's theory that Baskin killed her husband, Donald Lewis. But did she do it?

Unhappily Married

When she was 17, Baskin began dating her boss, Michael Murdock. The relationship moved fast. After just a few months of dating, she moved into his house in 1979. Despite her parents' disapproval of the relationship, the pair married shortly after they started cohabitating.

The marriage was tumultuous. Murdock complained about Baskin's lack of motivation; she complained about his sex drive. After just a few months of marriage, Baskin announced that she was having a baby. Their daughter was born on July 16, 1980.

Murdock and his wife continued to argue about everything. As the relationship deteriorated, Baskin found comfort in the arms of another man. One Donald Lewis. He was also married, which only seemed to fuel the passion more.

Baskin encouraged Lewis to divorce his wife, and she would leave Murdock. During her divorce, she accused her husband of abuse. He countered with allegations of her infidelity.

After contentious divorces, Lewis and Baskin were free to be together. She had an eye for real estate, which is an area that her new love had been quite fond of. Together they grew his fortune.

The relationship was not a happy one, though. Once again, Baskin found herself with a man who loved sex. Lewis, however, did not like sex with his girlfriend. He had lovers all over, including in Costa Rica.

The couple was not happy.

Easy Street Fight
Even with unhappiness seeping into their relationship, Baskin and Lewis continued on. In 1991, they got married. They also started Wildlife On Easy Street, which would later be renamed Big Cat Rescue.

It is believed that Lewis helped her start the nonprofit to move her out of the real estate company. He liked having the opportunity to be with his lovers without his wife being around.

Baskin would acknowledge this. She told friends that Lewis would plan his trips to Costa Rica for when she was menstruating. It did not seem to bother her much.

But Lewis began to let his loved ones know how unhappy he was with her. He recounted how abusive she was and the threats that were made against his life. In July 1997, he was so worried about his wife's erratic behavior, he filed for a restraining order. Baskin denied the charges.

She claimed he only went to court because of a spat they had. While he was in Costa Rica, she moved some of his belongings out of the house. Still, Lewis's actions put his family on edge. They feared something would happen to him.

Then Donald Lewis changed his will and didn't tell anyone. Allegedly.

Gone Husband
Less than a month after Lewis filed for a restraining order, he went missing. On August 18, 1997, He was supposed to make an early morning delivery and then head to Costa Rica for a business trip. Baskin reported her husband missing the next day.

Police thought they were on to something when they found his 1989 Dodge Ram van. It was parked at the Pilot County Airport, about 40 miles from where Lewis and Baskin lived. The keys for the van were on the dashboard. There were no other clues.

Investigators flew to Costa Rica when Baskin told them he may have gone there to start a new life. He wasn't there. They did find that he enjoyed the company of other people often. There were also allegations of illegal business practices.

Back in the United States, Baskin was putting together a plan to have Lewis declared dead. She began closing down the real estate company, even though she did not own it legally.

After five years, on August 19, 2002, Donald Lewis was declared legally dead. Instantly there was a fight over the will. Lewis's daughters from his first marriage believed that Baskin was trying to circumvent their father's wishes.

Indeed, they fought over the estate. A judge awarded Basking the bulk of Lewis's assets. After the decision was handed down, she cut her former husband's children out of her life.

She blamed them for taking her to court. They accused her of killing their father.

Allegations Pile Up
As time went on, the urgency to find out what happened to Don Lewis has faded. While the case is still open, there were no active investigations into his disappearance. Until Tiger King became a phenomenon.

Ever since the show debuted, the police department has been given tips every single day. The belief is that a disgruntled former employee will come forward with information about what happened.

One item that came to light due to the renewed interest in the case was concerning the will. Hillsborough County Sheriff Chad Chronister revealed that there is no doubt the will was forged. He even went as far as to say the signature was clumsily traced. However, because the statute of limitations had expired, no charges could be filed.

It added fuel to the fire of Baskin's guilt, though. Lewis's daughters decided to step up the fight and offer a reward for information leading to the arrest of Carole Baskin for the murder of her husband.

A group of people uncovered more evidence that casts doubt on her innocence. There was a theory that she had placed her husband's body in a septic tank. She denied this charge and claimed that the tank had been installed long after Lewis went missing.

However, a group found the receipts for the septic tank. It was installed shortly after he went missing. Which has caused police to reexamine the evidence they had collected before.

Joe Maldonado-Passage theorized in a song that Baskin fed her husband to a cat. She denies any wrongdoing or knowing anything about Lewis's disappearance.

But she does love her cats.

CHAPTER SIXTEEN

Secrets Of A Comedy Legend

\ Onscreen Bob Crane was known as a talented comedian, able to milk a joke for all it was worth. Offscreen he harbored a secret life that shocked fans as it slowly came out in the tabloids. The secret helped usher in the end of his career.

It also helped bring an end to his second marriage. Crane had grown weary of his wife. They were constantly arguing about things. One of the fiercest fights they had was about the comedian always being on the road. She wanted him to be at home with her. He wanted to save his career.

While working on staging a dinner theatre play, Crane was murdered. It is a mystery that rattled Hollywood and set up a family feud. While no one had ever been brought to justice for the murder, there have been many attempts at solving it.

Who wanted Bob Crane dead and why?

Heroes Welcome

Crane began his career as a radio host. During his tenure at L.A.'s KNX, he interviewed stars like Marilyn Monroe and Carl Reiner. It was the latter guest who thought of Crane for a guest role on The Dick Van Dyke Show. He was tasked with playing a philandering husband.

The spot was such a hit that it led to a series regular role on The Donna Reed Show. Once again, Crane stole the show. Audiences loved the burgeoning star. They watched the show in record numbers to see what shenanigans his character would get up to. Every producer of a sitcom wanted to sign him.

As his tenure on The Donna Reed Show wound down, his agent began sending him scripts. One of them was the pilot for Hogan's Heroes. The former radio host loved the story but thought it was a drama, so he asked his agent why it had been sent to him. It was explained to him that despite it being set in World War II Germany, the show would be a comedy.

He signed almost immediately.

Crane and his first wife, Anne Terzian, celebrated. Though the highs of the moment would be fleeting. The show was a hit right away, something unheard of in the 1960s.

But it afforded Crane the luxury of indulging in his favorite passion: women. During the filming of the first season, he had a fling with costar Cynthia Lynn. The affair ended, and she was written off the show.

Patricia Olson was brought on to play a similar role on the show. She also had an affair with Crane. This relationship brought an end to Crane's first marriage.

The liaisons with his costars were not the only time Crane stepped outside of his marriage for companionship.

Complicated Lives

As the popularity of Hogan's Heroes exploded, Crane found more women who were willing to indulge him. He befriended John Henry Carpenter, a sales manager for Sony Electronics. His new friend helped him pick out camcorders and other recording equipment.

The sitcom star had taken a liking to recording himself having sex with women. These tapes were not shared with anyone else. And the women who appeared in the movies consented to be recorded. Everyone seemed to be happy with the arrangement.

Everyone that is but Olson.

After Crane divorced Terzian, he quickly married his mistress. When she learned that he was cheating on her, she was furious. This led to arguments about what marriage should look like.

Olson blamed Carpenter for her husband's philandering. She felt the camera salesman was a bad influence and wanted to wedge him out of their lives. Crane did not agree with her. He and his buddy continued to spend nights looking for ladies at nightclubs.

When he didn't record the women he went to bed with, Crane took polaroids of them. He then put together books to show off to his buddies. While he filmed the Disney movie, Superdad, Crane passed around the books he had created. Word leaked to The National Enquirer, and they ran the story.

Crane's career in Hollywood went up in smoke. And so did his second marriage.

Descent Of A Sitcom Legend

The scandal rocked Crane's bosses. While they publicly coalesced around him privately, they decided to end the show. And with that decision, the offers that had once poured in disappeared.

He was offered guest spots on shows like The Love Boat. However, there were no high paying gigs that had been expected as his hit sitcom came to an end. Executives felt that he would be toxic to their brands, which were by and large family-friendly.

Ever inventive and resourceful, Crane began doing dinner theatre. He enjoyed it so much that he bought the rights to a play, Beginners Luck. He set up a workshop for the show in Scottsdale, Arizona.

Before he was killed, Crane called his son, Robert. Their conversation had a hopeful tone. The former sitcom star told his namesake that he was making changes. He was ditching Carpenter as a friend, and he was divorcing Olson. A clean start was what he wanted, and this was his way of getting it.

Olson felt differently. She had put up with his cheating and endured the scandal with him. There was no way she was going to go silently into the night as Terzian had.

Neither would Carpenter. The night Crane was killed, the two men were seen at a restaurant arguing. It is believed that the salesman did not take kindly to the ending of his friendship with the star.

Hours after the dinner, Crane's head was bashed in, and a cord was wrapped around his neck.

No Justice For Crane
When police responded to a call about the noise at Crane's rented apartment, they were shocked by what was found. The corpse was in such bad shape that they could not identify it. Instead, they went

through the leasing office and confirmed with the Windmill Dinner Theatre that it was the former sitcom star.

The investigation focused on Carpenter. It was believed that he had been upset by Crane's decision to discontinue their friendship. Blood in his car and on his clothes further fueled the speculation that he had something to do with the murder. However, no murder weapon was uncovered, and for many years the prosecutor refused to press charges at the time.

However, another detective picked up the case in 1991. While reviewing the evidence, he found a photograph of Carpenter's car. Upon closer inspection, a speck of brain was found. A judge ruled the new evidence was admissible.

It was the break everyone had hoped for.

John Henry Carpenter was charged with the murder of his former friend Bob Crane. Just as it seemed like there would be justice for the fallen star, it fell away. The defense successfully argued that the murderer might have been an angry boyfriend or husband of a woman that Crane bedded. They also pointed out that the murder weapon was not found. Carpenter was acquitted.

With the prime suspect cleared, it seemed as though the case would never be solved.

New Suspects
Many still believe that Carpenter was the one who ended Crane's life. Phoenix reporter John Hook was granted permission to run DNA tests on evidence in 2016. After this was done, he had hoped to be able to name Carpenter as the real killer. However, the results came back inconclusive.

Robert Crane has suggested that his stepmother may have been behind the murder. Since the elder Crane had been in the middle of divorcing Olson, she had a motive. Once the marriage was legally ended, she would no longer have access to her husband's money. With him being dead, she had unfettered rights to the cash.

Fueling the theory were some of the moves she made after his death. After he was buried with other family members, Olson had Crane's body dug up and moved to a cemetery. A decision that she did not tell her husband's older children about.

She also set up a website. Ostensibly it was to celebrate the life of a beloved Hollywood figure. However, Olson began selling the amateur porn that Crane had made. Without the consent of the women involved. Someone complained about this, and the website was quickly shut down.

Carpenter died in 1998. Olson died in 2007.

Leaving many to wonder if this is one of the mysteries that will go into the annals of Hollywood's unsolved mysteries.

CHAPTER SEVENTEEN

Curious Case Trailer Park Boys

Fans of the show *Trailer Park Boys* have debated why one of the stars left. Some believed Lucy DeCoutere's account of what happened. Others argue she was fired.

DeCoutere says that she left because a costar allegedly beat his significant other; fans are saying bull and alleging that she was let go because of her performance.

Facts Are Facts

Netflix bought and rebooted the series in 2014. Two years later, Mike Smith was arrested in Los Angeles on charges of domestic abuse. However, his lady friend Georgia Ling released a statement saying that she never felt threatened and that other people called the police. Here is part of Ling's statement: "The police were called by others not present in the room who mistakenly perceived the argument to be something other than what it was. When the officers arrived, I tried to assure them there was no real issue, but they proceeded to arrest Mike." Some wondered if Ling really felt that way or if someone had put her up to releasing that statement.

Producers of the Netflix hit supported their star. On the Trailer Park Boy's Facebook page, there are statements from both Ling and Smith: "The other members of the Trailer Park Boys and all staff stand behind Mike and look forward to the matter being resolved favourably." It makes sense that they are treating this as an 'innocent until proven guilty' situation, especially with Ling saying that nothing happened. Only Smith and Ling were in the room, so they are the only ones who know what happened.

Co-Star Debate
Even with that being the case, Lucy DeCoutere decided to get involved and let people know that she thinks her costar is guilty. In a series of tweets, she let it all out. "If I find out that somebody is abusive, I cut them out of my life. It's very easy, I have resigned from Trailer Park Boys." Fans were quick to pounce and point out that her departure from the show happened before the alleged incident.

That is what fans are thinking happened. In fact, quite a few of them are commenting and re-posting comments like this:

"...All witnesses involved in the incident (including the victim) have already stated that there was no physical assault involved, just a lot of yelling by both parties involved. 3. This is how she treats a co-worker of 15 years? Without even hearing out the details? Just an excuse to leave a job before she would be terminated, then pin it on someone or something else. Zero credibility."

Bolstering the case of DeCoutere is that Smith was accused of sexual assault in 2019. In 2005, a young woman alleged that Smith plied her with alcohol in a club and took her home. He forced her into having sex with him. Reportedly she talked with the police about the incident, but they said she could be in trouble for being in the club while underaged. She was 18 at the time of the incident; the legal drinking age in Canada is 19.

Fired, Resigned, Or Forced Out?
DeCourtere says that she resigned, and official statements seem to support that. However, in the entertainment industry, many people are allowed to say they quit instead of being terminated.

Many think she was terminated because Smith is part owner of the Trailer Park Boys franchise. The two had allegedly had a falling out before the Ling allegations. It is believed DeCourtere was on her way out already and needed a reason why she would be leaving a hit show, making a lot of money.

It is not likely the truth will come out. And even unlikelier that Smith will pay for alleged abuses.

CHAPTER EIGHTEEN

Unfair Trial Of A Confessed Outlaw

Charles Harrelson was the last of the classic American hitman. That's how one former friend described the convicted killer. Harrelson claimed to have killed 50 people. His friend countered that it was probably only five or six murders, though he conceded that the hitman could have participated in other hit jobs.

One of Harrelson's claims was that he was part of President John F. Kennedy's assassination. Conspiracy theorists have embraced his words and believe that he was one of the "three tramps." The FBI investigated his story but determined that it was nothing more than a fabrication. .

Harrelson was tied to the 1968 murder of a Texas man, Alan Berg. It was alleged that the hitman had been hired to kill Berg because of his gambling debt. While Harrelson was acquitted of the murder, he later confessed that he had been the one who took out the young man.

Later in 1968, he would stand accused of murder once again. Sam Degelia Jr. was a grain dealer and in business with his best friend, Pete Thomas Scamardo. However, Scamardo was trafficking heroin with Harrelson. He also happened to be deeply in debt and wanted Degelia out of the way so he could collect a life insurance policy on him.

After Degelia was killed, Harrelson was seen around town. He was arrested and tried for the murder. After a short trial, the jury was deadlocked. A second trial saw him convicted of the crime. He was sentenced to 15 years in prison.

This was not his only conviction.

The Judge Is Out

After serving five years, Harrelson was paroled for good behavior. He embraced his freedom by marrying his latest lady love, Jo-Ann Harrelson. After the wedding, he also reconnected with his friend Jamiel Chagra, a drug dealer. They talked about the good old days, and Chagra began talking about a possible job he had for the hitman.

U.S. District Judge John H. Wood was the target. Wood was known as a tough sentencer; he would give out maximum prison terms for drug dealers. Chagra was supposed to appear before him after being convicted of trafficking drugs.

Wood was assassinated on the morning that the sentencing had initially been scheduled to take place. A last-minute delay had pushed back the court date, but the plan had been put into motion and could not be stopped.

Police got a tip that Harrelson was responsible for the murder and arrested him. They began to piece together a case against him. Witnesses claimed that he had been in the area of the judge's townhouse. But there was no physical evidence against him.

Jamiel Chagra went to visit his brother, Joe, in jail. They talked about Jamiel hiring Harrelson to assassinate the judge; he bragged that it was the perfect way to avoid a lengthy prison sentence. Everything seemed to be going his way.

Unbeknownst to them, their conversation was being taped by the police. The confession was used to paint Harrelson as a dangerous man, a cold-blooded killer.

The prosecutor's case rested solely on this piece of evidence.

Guilty Or Not

As the trial got underway, Harrelson's lawyers argued the jailhouse conversation was taped illegally. They wanted it thrown out and deemed inadmissible in court. The judge ruled against them with convoluted reasoning.

Prosecutors charged both of the Chagra brothers with the assassination of Judge Wood as well. Joe was convicted alongside Harrelson for the murder in the case. Jamiel was acquitted because his brother would not testify against him. He did testify against the hitman. There were claims that Harrelson bragged about the payday for the murder.

After the jury returned their verdict, the judge handed down two life sentences to Harrelson. He appealed the conviction, citing that the conversation between Joe and Jamiel had been illegally recorded. There were also claims of improper conduct by prosecutors. None of the arguments worked.

In 2003, Jamiel Chagra was released from prison. The first thing he did was tell people that Harrelson was not the person who killed Wood. He claimed that he knew the police were recording his conversation with his brother and wanted to set the hitman up.

Harrelson had been blackmailing Joe Chagra with some information he had on the murder. The brothers cooked up the plot to pin the murder on him.

The story wasn't enough to get a new trial for Harrelson. Appeals judges were not interested in listening to someone who was a known criminal and a self-professed liar.

Confessions From The Grave

On July 4, 1995, Harrelson and two other prisoners attempted to escape from prison. They were caught by guards watching in the prisoner's tower. A warning shot was fired, and the trio surrendered.

After the incident, Harrelson was moved to a super-maximum security prison in Florida. He began to write his life story and compiled stories from his life. Friends and family asked if he was doing alright, he assured them that he was. His one complaint was that there were not enough hours in the day.

Nobody was quite sure what his mysterious project was. He had divorced Jo-Ann after the conviction. Another lady caught his attention, but he hadn't revealed what he was working on for a long while.

Finally, he told his son, actor Woody Harrelson. He talked about how he wanted to get his story out in the open. He claimed that people needed to know about the dark forces that were trying to shape the government and protect the mafia.

Harrelson was found dead in his cell on March 15, 2007. Sometime during the night, he had suffered a heart attack. When the family collected his belongings, they were shocked to find a binder full of handwritten notes.

They served as the beginnings of the memoir he had wanted to write. Woody Harrelson has said he is not sure what to do with the papers yet.

Many stories could open old wounds for families.

In The End... It Didn't Matter

The stories in the papers included several confessions. Harrelson admitted to killing Delegia and Berg. He shared details that only the killer would have known about the crimes. There was also an apology for ripping the men away from their loved ones.

He also doubled down on his claim to have been at the scene when President Kennedy was assassinated. Once again, he included details that pointed to his presence at the scene. Multiple investigators also claim that there are pictures of him being there.

When it came to Judge Wood, he emphatically denied being the murderer.

Woody Harrelson tried to get a posthumous reversal for his father. It did not work.

But Charles Harrelson will be forever remembered as the last of the American criminals. His legacy of murder, mayhem, and a rigged trial will be remembered for lifetimes to come.

CHAPTER NINETEEN

Controversial Night Out For Soul Singer

Sam Cooke was known to the world as the godfather of soul. He popularized the genre with a string of top 10 hits that spoke to the American youth in the 1950s and 1960s. His success opened the door for other acts to follow him.

As with many celebrities, Cooke's personal life was fascinating. He married his first wife, Dolores Elizabeth Milligan, in 1953. The marriage was tense and unhappy because of the singer's inability to say no to other women. Cooke and Milligan agreed to divorce in 1958.

Shortly after his first divorce, Cooke married his second wife, Barbara Campbell. This union seemed to be more stable. Campbell turned her head when rumors of her husband's infidelities bubbled up. She stood by his side when Milligan was killed in a car accident a year after they wed. When he paid for the funeral, she thought it was a good deed.

Even as other women came forward with stories of being with Cooke, Campbell said nothing. When one lady claimed Cooke was the father of her child, Campbell encouraged her husband to pay the woman in an out of court settlement.

The relationship puzzled those who watched it. Things became more apparent when it was revealed that Campbell had a penchant for sleeping with other men.

Night Out At Hacienda

On December 10, 1964, Cooke was celebrating his latest success. His album, Live At The Copa, was racing up the charts. He was crossing over into the big leagues, there were favorable comparisons to Sammy Davis Jr. and Nat King Cole. Martinis and other alcohol were flowing freely.

Cooke was having dinner at Martoni's Italian Restaurant with Al and Joan Schmitt. Fans and other admirers would stop by the table and congratulate the singer on the success he was having. A few people asked for his autograph.

A group of friends pulled Cooke into the bar area of the restaurant. He sang along with the music and danced with his pals. They would comment on a couple of the ladies that made their way through the bar. One of the women caught the singer's eye.

She sat at the bar, sipping on her drink. Every so often, she would look over at Cooke and smile slyly at him. One of Cooke's pals noticed the flirting and introduced the two.

The woman was Elisa Boyer. As the night progressed, the two became closer. Another man tried to flirt with the lady, but Cooke let him know that she was spoken for.

Cooke and Boyer climbed into his Ferrari. She has claimed that she asked him to take her home, but the singer refused. Instead, they sped down the freeway. He pulled the car into the parking lot of Hacienda Motel.

A tragic mistake.

The Room Where It Happened

Cooke pulled the car into a spot and went into the hotel. He went in and talked with the manager, Bertha Franklin. During their encounter, he flashed a wad of cash and slid a few bills over. The register showed that Cooke gave his real name.

Franklin eyed Boyer in the car and forced the singer to add her to the register as his wife. Once they were finished, the manager handed Cooke the key to the room.

The singer climbed into the car and pulled it around to the front of the building. Boyer and Cooke went into the room. She claims that he began pawing at her, tearing off her clothes. At some point, she was able to get away from him and went to the bathroom. The window was painted shut.

When she went back into the room, Cooke was naked. He pushed her onto the bed. At the last minute, he went to the bathroom himself. Boyer grabbed her clothes, as well as his, and ran out of the room. She claimed that she didn't mean to grab his clothes.

Boyer knocked on Franklin's door first, but there was no answer. She was about half a block from the hotel when she ditched Cooke's clothing. The cash that had been in his pockets was not found.

Cooke ran out of the room naked, with the exception of one shoe and a sports coat. He went to Franklin's room and pounded on the door. Several people claimed he heard him scream about the girl being in the place with Franklin. When she didn't answer the door, he kicked it in.

Bertha Franklin was ready for him.

Struggle And Investigation
The fight started the minute Cooke was inside the manager's room. There were shouts and obscenities between the two. Accusations of misconduct were also exchanged.

As Cooke made his way into the room, he started looking for Boyer. Franklin tried to push him out, going as far as to pull a gun on him. This led the two to a physical fight. The motel manager admitted to the police that she bit him.

When she reached for the gun, Cooke noticed it and tried to grab it as well. Franklin got control of the gun and fired shots into the man point-blank. The police arrived with the paramedics.

Sam Cooke was pronounced dead on the scene.

Barbara Cooke (nee Campbell) was informed of her husband's death at six in the morning. She was not surprised that he was with another woman.

The police investigated the murder for five days. Boyer and Franklin testified before a jury of seven. Boyer continued to claim that Cooke had kidnapped her and planned on raping her.

Franklin argued that he broke into her room. Given that, her shooting was self-defense. She claimed to have feared for her safety and had no idea why Cooke had come to her when Boyer left.

The answer was right under the surface and would be exposed soon.

However, it was too late. The jury found that Cooke's murder was justified homicide, and the case was closed.

Truth Revealed Slowly

Cooke's family was not content with the findings of the police or jury. They believed that the singer had been killed for nefarious reasons. His mother thought that someone in Hollywood's elite wanted to take out the rising black star. While his wife believed Boyer and Franklin worked together to rob him of his money. And there was evidence of this being the case.

Boyer's charge of kidnapping was immediately dismissed by police. While it made sense that she would not jump out of a moving car, there were plenty of opportunities for her to run away while Cooke was paying for the hotel room. Police dismissed her charges out of hand, especially after they looked at her rap sheet. Which was about to grow longer.

Less than a month after Cooke's murder, Boyer was arrested for prostitution. It was revealed that she was familiar with Hacienda Motel, as she had been busted as a sex worker there before. Many noted that she was quite close to Bertha Franklin.

Miss Franklin had her own set of criminal charges. She was a well-known madam who was always fighting with the law. After being cleared of the murder, she sued Cooke's estate for $200,000, but the case was dismissed.

It is widely believed that Franklin and Boyer cooked up a plot to rob the singer, as Barbara Cooke suggested. Mostly as the money he had in his pockets disappeared.

CHAPTER TWENTY

What Happens On The Show Affects Real Life

Daniela Perez and Guilherme de Pádua shared a steamy kiss. The crew of their hit telenovela, De Corp e Alama, watched as the two actors pulled away from one another. The director yelled, cut and there was scattered applause for the duo.

With the cameras off, de Pádua stormed away from his co-star. Audiences loved the chemistry between the pair. However, he felt as though he were being slighted by the show's producers. He wanted more storylines and to be considered the heart of the show.

As the weeks wore on, the mood on the set grew darker. Producers had grown weary of de Pádua's antics behind the scenes, the diva fits he threw. They gathered to talk about how to deal with the situation. There was a clause in his contract that allowed for them to fire him with or without cause.

Since his character was involved in a popular romantic storyline with Perez, producers decided to wait. It was a choice they came to regret. De Pádua started telling crew members that he and Perez were having an affair off-screen as well. Those rehearsals were a guise for their affair.

Word got back to the producers, who decided this was cause for termination. They also began cutting scenes that featured de Pádua and Perez together. A story was devised to cut his run on the show short.

De Pádua did not like this plan.

A Twisted Marriage

While he was busy creating tension on set, de Pádua was not fairing better at home. His wife, Paula Nogueira Thomaz, noted that he had not been as affectionate with her. The couple argued about what was happening; neither wanted the relationship to come to an end.

Then as he learned his time on the telenovela was coming to an end, he stunned his wife with a confession. He cheated on her with Daniela Perez. The affair started innocently, with them rehearing. But she could not keep her hands off the married man, and he succumbed to her feminine wiles.

De Pádua went one step further. He told his wife that Perez wanted to take their affair public. But since her career was on the rise, the only way it would work is if he left Thomaz to be with her.

Rather than being mad, Thomaz informed her husband that he knew what needed to be done. Near the beginning of their relationship, they made a pact: should de Pádua cheat on her, he would kill his lover.

Thomaz explained that before they agreed to be married, they consulted with a black magic priest. The "religious" leader told them a fidelity promise would make their union much stronger. It would also prove to be a deterrent to affairs.

Since it didn't work, Thomaz insisted that de Pádua kill Perez.

The Truth About Daniela Perez

Daniela Perez went about her business as usual as the de Pádua played itself out. While her affair rumors made their way back to her, she wasn't concerned about them. After a meeting with the producers, she was comforted with the knowledge that her co-star would soon be off the show. Once that happened, the lies would stop.

De Pádua and Thomaz ambushed Perez on December 28, 1992. An argument ensued about the relationship between the castmates. Perez denied having an affair with the married man. Thomaz did not believe her romantic rival.

They stabbed her 18 times. The weapon punctured her lungs, heart, and neck. She died instantly.

Police discovered her body and began to compile a list of suspects. The investigation led them to ask her former colleagues if anyone had a reason to harm the beloved star.

People began spilling about de Pádua, boasting that he was having an affair with Perez. Officers took note and asked if the affair had ended badly. They were stunned by the answer.

Perez and de Pádua never had an affair. She was married, and her husband often came to the set to see his beloved wife. Most of the crew believed he claimed to have an affair hoping that it would leak to the tabloids and cement his spot on the show.

Gloria Perez, the show's head writer, and Daniela's mother informed the police that nothing would save de Pádua's role. The decision to fire had already been made.

Police decided to bring in Thomaz and de Pádua for questioning.

Turning On The Other

As police worked on bringing the married couple into the station, they continued their investigation. The piece of the puzzle that confused them was why de Pádua claimed to have an affair with Perez when it was clear he didn't.

An answer came to them in the form of a psychologist. The expert theorized that the actor could not differentiate between real life and the storylines on the telenovela. It seemed like a wild hypothesis, but there was enough validity in it that they tested it out.

When de Pádua came in for questioning, they asked him some questions about Perez's affair inspired by their character's storyline. His answers matched up with what happened onscreen.

As the questions continued, the actor surprised detectives. He admitted to being there when Perez was murdered. However, he was not the culprit; his wife did it. Thomaz was jealous of his affair and wanted her romantic rival out of the way, so she stabbed her with a screwdriver.

Down the hall, Thomaz also confessed to being there for the murder. She claimed her husband stabbed his alleged mistress with scissors. When she was pressed further, she admitted that she had stabbed the woman too, but contended her husband dealt the fatal blow.

Thomaz later recanted her statement.

De Pádua and his wife were charged with second-degree murder.

Out In A Flash

Thomaz and de Pádua were tried separately. Each built a defense around the other being the murderer. They hoped to confuse the juries, and it would lead to an acquittal for both.

They were disappointed when both juries convicted them. Each received a sentence of 19 years. Thomaz was released shortly before her husband. Controversy arose because they only served 6 years of their sentence.

Gloria Perez and Daniela's widower sued the couple after they were released from prison. The case bounced around the courts until it was finally taken before a jury. The victim's loved ones were awarded $440,000 each.

Thomaz remarried and has largely stayed out of the limelight.

Her now ex-husband also remarried. De Pádua quit acting and became a minister. He avoids answering questions about his former co-star and murder victim.

A twist no one saw coming.

CHAPTER TWENTY-ONE

The Twinkling Star Who Made A Big Splash

When Natalie Wood dated Elvis Presley in September 1956, the world watched in fascination. Both stars were at the top of their careers. There seemed to be a genuine affection between the pair. But the relationship was not destined to last long.

Shortly after Wood broke up with Presley, she began a whirlwind relationship with Robert Wagner. The couple was passionate about one another. Love consumed them, and they decided to get married as soon as possible.

On December 28, 1957, less than a year after going public with their relationship, Wagner and Wood were married. While they maintained an image of a happy marriage, a much different story played out behind the scenes.

Both of their careers were in overdrive, so they barely spent any time together. When they were together, they argued about nearly everything. Cheating allegations flew back and forth between the superstar couple.

One of the fights was about infidelity. Wagner thought his wife was having affairs with her costars. Whiles Woods believed her husband allowed groupies onto the set of his movies to woo them.

As quickly as they married, they separated. Wood and Wagner's divorce was finalized on April 27, 1962, just over 4 years after their wedding.

Back To Love
Wood rebounded from the failed marriage with a quick succession of flings. She dated actors like Warren Beatty and Michael Caine. But it was shoe manufacturer Ladislav Blatnik that captured her heart.

The engagement was short-lived. Wood broke up with her fiancé in 1965.

In 1966, Wood met her next husband, Richard Gregson. The couple wed on May 30, 1969. As with her other unions, this marriage was stormy. Each had a different view of how marriage should be.

However, it was not all arguments and unhappiness. Wood gave birth to their daughter, Natasha, in 1970. But the baby was not enough to save the relationship, as they had hoped.

After two years of marriage, Wood filed for divorce.

The popular actress briefly dated politician Jerry Brown.

However, it was Wagner that caught her eye again. They had come full circle and began dating again in 1972, months before her divorce was finalized. The tumultuous duo wasted no time in remarrying.

Their second wedding happened on a yacht. Family and friends clapped as the couple exchanged vows. It seemed this time; they would be able to make it work.

Until accusations of infidelity began again.

One of the first marriage issues was Wood catching her husband in the throes of passion with another man. A charge that Wagner has vehemently denied over the years.

During their second marriage, Wood had an affair with an FBI agent. The man revealed their relationship started in 1973, shortly after her wedding, and ended in 1977.

More arguments over cheating would ensue. And one would end the superstar actress's life.

Woods In The Ocean
On the night of November 28, 1981, Wood was with her husband and close friend, Christopher Walken. The trio had taken a weekend away from work and taking some much-needed relaxation. They made the trek to Catalina Island and were on board Wagner's yacht, Splendour.

Wood suffered from seasickness, so she took medicine to help combat it. Her sickness got the best of her, and she went to lie down. Wagner and Walken continued to drink and party.

When Wagner joined her in their room, a fight ensued. Wood was heard asking him for a divorce and demanding to be taken back to shore. Her husband mocked her illness.

After the argument, Wagner went back to the main deck. He continued drinking with his buddy. The two didn't seem to notice Wood did not rejoin them.

Later that evening, Wood reportedly caught her husband and Walken in bed together. This led to another argument and more threats of divorce. She warned him that she would not keep the secret of his indiscretions this time.

After the fight, Wood ended up in the Pacific Ocean.

Dennis Davern, the boat captain, heard something fall into the water but never searched for who or what it was.

Wood's body was found at 8 am on November 29, 1981. Police tried to piece together what happened but were met with lies and stonewalling from Davern, Wagner, and Walken.

Because her blood alcohol level was 0.14 and there were traces of a painkiller, as well as the seasickness medicine, Wood's death was ruled an accident.

This designation would change.

Unlocking The Unsolved Mystery
Wood's death made continuous headlines for years. A new wrinkle seemed to be revealed every so often, usually to a tabloid publication. While the police seemed definitive in their conclusion, others kept digging into what happened on that fateful night.

Davern publicly stated that he lied to the police in 2011. This was enough for a detective to take a second look at the case, with new testimony from the former captain and evidence that appeared to be ignored from the investigators who initially handled the case.

There were unexplained bruises on the superstar's body. There was an abrasion on her face; none of the marks had been investigated or questioned by any of the officers.

Further shocking, the new detectives on the case was what the autopsy showed. Urine levels in Wood's body indicated that she was unconscious before she drowned.

These shockers were followed by a possible motive for Wagner to kill his wife. The FBI agent, who Wood had an affair with, revealed details of their dalliance publicly.

Adding a new layer and possible new motive was the revelation that Wood told her best friends, sister, and mother about catching Wagner with another man. She came home one day early and caught him fooling around with their butler.

Wagner fought back against these allegations. Though his arguments only served to prove his deception on the night his wife died.

Unanswered Questions
Investigators asked Walken to come in for questioning. He lawyered up and agreed. The interrogation went off without a hitch. After it happened, the police announced publicly that he was not a person of interest in the case.

Wagner refused to speak to the police. This led them to label him a person of interest in the case. He continues to proclaim his innocence. The widower says what happened the night Wood died was a horrible accident. One that changed his family.

He began dating Jill St. John shortly after Wood drowned. It has left many wondering why he moved on so quickly if he intended to stay married to the late actress.

The night Natalie Wood died remains a mystery. But new information emerges every year about what happened.

CHAPTER TWENTY-TWO
Perfect Storm For Murder

It's a running joke in the entertainment industry that reality shows aren't so real. They may not employ scriptwriters to create drama; producers meddle in situations and outcomes for the best drama. Even if it's not what the participant wants to do.

What happens if the producers meddle too much and steer things off course? The producers of Megan Wants A Millionaire found out the hard way. They cast Ryan Jenkins, who appeared on another reality show the company produced. Producers tampered with the results of Megan; they ended up with two deaths to their credit.

The ensuing murder case also exposed how much control producers have over the shows and how things work out.

Reality Works
In the late aughts, celebreality shows were the hottest thing, especially on the Viacom owned VH1. After they had success with The Surreal Life, they were hungry for more of those types of shows. The production company, 51 Minds Entertainment, was more than happy to develop content for the media giant.

Megan Hauserman appeared on The Surreal Life and placed third. One of the "fun" aspects of Hauserman was her relentless belief that she should end up with a man who was worth millions. Producers thought it would make a fun reality show and set about pitching the spinoff. VH1 execs loved the idea and bought it right off the bat.

The casting process was supposed to be rigorous, and for most of the contestants, it was. However, Ryan Jenkins was able to pass the background check with his arrest for domestic assault, never being known to producers or to Hauserman. He joined the cast.

But nobody saw what happened next coming.

Too Real Reality

Hauserman admits that she liked Jenkins. There were some red flags that she chose to ignore. One of them was that he brought only one pair of pants for a five-week shoot. The other was that he only wore fake Rolex watches. Still, despite these warnings about his financial status, the former Playboy model was smitten with him.

She liked him so much that she began having a relationship with him via the phone. They would take after filming ended for the day. At one point, she told him that he would be the one she chose at the end of the day. That was the plan, at least.

As producers started to realize what was happening, they knew they needed to do something. Jenkins was fun as a villain and a possible spoiler, but his winning would not please the audience. It would mean fewer people would watch the planned season 2 of the show. They reached out to Hauserman and told her of their problem. She claims that they asked her to send him home early to make better TV.

Hauserman planned to let Jenkins know once the season was over what really happened. But she was too late. Jenkins had run off to Las Vegas and married another blonde-haired model. He told his former love that he had met his soulmate and they were very happy together.

Troubled Marriage

Except Jenkins and his new bride, Jasmine Fiore, weren't exactly enjoying their honeymoon. Right after the wedding, Jenkins was cast on I Love Money 3. He flew out to Mexico for the shoot.

Far from being an absent husband, he called Fiore every chance he got. He would then question where she was and what she had been doing. According to multiple sources, Jenkins was obsessed with his wife and convinced that she was cheating on him. She was, after all, in the city of sin without him.

Sources say that the couple would have huge fights about money and fidelity. It was part of the reason he had signed up for the second reality show. He kept assuring her he would win and bring home big money and give her the life he promised.

After filming, he went back to Vegas. But the reunion with his wife was short-lived. Fiore's mutilated body would be found on August 19, 2009. Her teeth and fingers had been removed. Investigators could only identify her body by the serial number on her breast implants.

Investigating the Investigators

As the manhunt for Jenkins commenced, Viacom bosses were demanding answers. 51 Minds Entertainment had outsourced the background checks to a company called Collective Intelligence. The company had worked with Viacom and 51 Minds quite a bit, and there had never been an issue before. However, Jenkins was Canadian, and Collective Intelligence only did background checks for people in the United States.

So another company was brought in. Straightline International was supposed to do the check on Jenkins, but they dropped the ball. When execs at Collective Intelligence called, the people at Starightline dodged their calls. Eventually, the case would end in a breach of contract lawsuit.

In the meantime, Jenkins was on the run with the police hot on his trail. They would catch up to him. Unfortunately, he had taken his life before the cops were able to find him. He allegedly left behind a note.

Police say in the note Jenkins did not blame the murder of Fiore or even acknowledge her death. However, several family members came out and claimed that the former reality star had indeed admitted to the murder. It has never been released to the public.

Reality Fallout
Megan Wants A Millionaire was pulled off of VH1's schedule after just three episodes. The official website and page for the show were deleted. It was unofficially canceled. As was the entire season of I Love Money 3. 51 Minds took a huge financial hit, made even worse by the $12 million fine from Viacom and VH1 for the unused content.

Collective Intelligence also hit hard times financially. They laid off the entire staff as they regrouped. Execs were able to salvage the relationship with Viacom, though not without major concessions. They settled a lawsuit with Straightline International for $800,000.

The celebreality genre died within a year of this scandal. There have been a few attempts to resurrect it, but none have been truly fruitful.

CHAPTER TWENTY-THREE

The Signature Of An Election Spoiler

Kanye West announced his candidacy for president on Twitter. His declaration was not taken seriously by many people. They thought it was a publicity stunt for an upcoming album or project. He promised that was not the case; his bid for the highest office in the land was earnest.

The argument took a tumble during his search for a running mate. There were names like Joel Olsteen and Elon Musk thrown out, which furthered the idea that West was doing this for attention. Musk and Olsteen both objected to having their names in the mix.

West's wife, Kim Kardashian, further fueled the speculation that he was running for president as a stunt. She told the tabloid press that she wasn't aware of her husband's intentions until tweeting them out. Her fans spread the news and wondered aloud why he would announce his candidacy without talking to his spouse.

The answer seemed to come from Kardashian herself. She went on the record to multiple sources as being opposed to the notion of her husband running. Among her concerns was that their family would not be ready for the onslaught of attention a campaign would bring them. And she worried about her husband's mental health.

Under the best of conditions, a campaign is grueling. With the added concerns of West living with bipolar disorder, it makes a presidential run nearly impossible.

Kardashian's fears were soon realized.

Breakdown Wyoming

During a rally on July 19, 2020, West had a breakdown. He spoke about an abortion that his wife almost had, without going into specifics about why she thought the procedure was necessary.

Adding to the confusion, West began talking about Harriet Tubman. Rather than singing her praises, he alleged that she didn't free slaves. Instead, she forced the people she was saving to work with other white people.

Many people noted that it was his way of doubling down on a controversial claim he had made in the past. West believes that slaves chose the life of slavery. A position that was met with a backlash against the rapper.

Shortly after the rally, West announced the end of his candidacy. The political world sighed. It seemed the strangest addition to the field had exited. Pundits pontificated that the Grammy-winning rapper joined the race to fuel sales and interest in his latest album due to drop at the end of July.

Kardashian met with her husband in his Wyoming home. The couple was rumored to be at odds about many things, including the presidential campaign.

Word leaked out from the house that Kardashian asked West for a divorce. Their marriage was already strained, and this situation further exasperated the issues they faced.

Once his wife left, West invited members of the media into his house. He kept them waiting. When he joined them, he asked them not to mention anything that happened. He wanted to control the narrative of his marriage and campaign. They declined his request and were shown the door by his security team.

While this was playing out, sordid details of West's campaign were beginning to come out.

Reason To Run
West was surprised to learn that announcing his candidacy was not enough to get on the ballots. He changed his strategy to "walking" for president. He still insisted that he was in the race to win but acknowledged that it would be much harder for him to do that.

In an interview with Forbes, the Grammy winner admitted that his candidacy had ulterior motives. The hope was that he would siphon the black vote away from former Vice President Joe Biden and help Donald J. Trump win the election.

The reporter pointed out that West would not appear on many ballots. Shortly after the interview, West partnered up with GOP operatives to get his name on many state ballots. The people he hired were shady and had long histories of working outside of the law. Something that West didn't mind.

They began to collect signatures in states like New Jersey and Virginia. When questioned about why he was working with Republicans after denouncing the two-party system, West demurred.

He continued to hold his head down as the operatives began

collecting signatures to get him on the ballots. Stories about the group started to grow. People talked of how they were followed and shouted at when a voter declined to sign the petition.

Besides the strongarm tactics, no one believed West would be a significant factor in the race. After his first rally, he didn't hold anymore. And there were no ads or any sign that the rapper truly wanted to be the president.

An announcement shocked the people who planned on voting for West and changed the campaign's course for him.

Rap For Jail

New Jersey officials announced that of the 1,327 signatures that were turned in by West's campaign, more than 700 were thrown out. They didn't say why the signatures were thrown out, but an investigation was promised.

The same situation played out in Illinois. West's campaign submitted 2,500 signatures. Of the submitted signatures, only 1,200 were valid. Lawyers challenged the attempt to get on the ballot. The rapper confirmed he would likely not be able to be present on the form.

Election officials began to look into why the states tossed out so many signatures. In almost any petition, some designations are thrown out for reasons like the name is misspelled or not a registered voter. However, it seemed odd that there had been so many thrown out for one candidate.

Pundits began to speculate that Kanye West could end up in jail. Voter fraud laws are strict, and nothing that happened could be written off as something that he was not aware of.

Should authorities pursue charges, the Grammy winner would be facing felony charges. While an investigation is underway, no one is commenting on who its target is and how much trouble West could be in.

A few people believe that someone took advantage of a sick man. And Kanye West may end up in jail because of their political games.

CHAPTER TWENTY-FOUR

Femme Fatale's Spiderweb

Charlotte Kirk knew what she wanted. Her main goal was to be a movie star. Working as an actress was not enough for the ambitious young woman. Only the pinnacle of fame would do for her.

And she would do anything to attain it.

When she was 19, Charlotte visited New York City to network with industry types. The gambit paid off, and she was cast in Black Dog Red Dog, a film produced by Oscar nominee James Franco.

Instead of being her big break, the movie was not widely released, and her scene was cut from the final version of the film. Still, Charlotte tasted success. She was convinced her star-making role was just an audition away.

An Instagram post announced that she was heading to Los Angeles. She hoped that being in the city of angels would allow her to network more and land a significant role.

However, she ended up in a very significant relationship. In November 2012, Charlotte began dating billionaire James Packer. Her new love introduced her to his business partner, Brett Ratner.

James and Brett formed RatPac Entertainment. They negotiated a deal with Warner Brothers to fund a slate of 75 movies.

When Charlotte and James broke up, she remained on friendly terms with Brett. At least for a while.

A New Man In The Picture
At a networking event, Charlotte used her feminine wiles to try landing a role. One wife of an executive claimed to have caught the young actress in the throes of seducing her husband.

The same night, Charlotte met her next boyfriend, Joshua Newton. Despite the 20 year age difference between the two, they seemed to be smitten with one another.

Joshua wanted to make sure his new love was happy. He knew how important her career was to her, so he cast her in a movie he was making and a music video.

Not content to wait, Charlotte stayed in contact with Brett Ratner. Her hope was to be cast in one of the movies he was producing with Warner Brothers. He remained noncommittal but introduced her to an important man with the media company, Kevin Tsujihara.

Kevin was the CEO and Chairman of Warner Brothers.

He fell in lust with the young actress. The two shared a night of passion. Then another. An affair blossomed, but there were strings.

Charlotte wanted Kevin to get her cast in roles. When he didn't, she sent text messages pouting and insinuating that she would reveal their affair. Brett stepped in to help the beleaguered studio head.

The mega-producer informed Charlotte that sleeping with a studio executive was not the right way to secure roles. If that was her end goal, she needed to sleep with producers or directors.

As the realization that she wasn't about to get what she wanted dawned on her, Charlotte decided to make people pay.

Text With The Wind

Kevin began feeling the pressure from his lover. She started pushing him for more significant, better roles and for the heads of studios to call her agent back. When that didn't happen, she would text him, wondering what the hold up was.

He turned to Brett for help. There had to be a way to get Charlotte off his back, Kevin said to his associate. She was demanding things that were starting to gain attention from people who were asking questions.

Jumping into action, Brett reached out to the actress. He asked her to back off Kevin and let things happen naturally. Forcing people to help her would not get her the career she wanted. Charlotte countered that the relationship with Kevin was not consensual and blamed Brett for it.

She claimed that the mega-producer used her to make sure the financing deal with Warner Brothers went through. Brett denied the allegation in a series of text messages to the actress. Charlotte held firm in her accusations.

The two engaged in a text war. Neither side budged in their belief. Charlotte claimed that Brett used her to get the signatures on the deal several times, with his denials coming in just as fast and furious.

When several women came forward and accused Brett Ratner of sexual assault, Charlotte saw her opening. She threatened to go to the press and tell her story.

Brett warned her that she was extorting him and that it was illegal. She denied that she was blackmailing anyone. But she did have her lawyer draw up a settlement that required Kevin and Brett to get her six auditions and guarantee her a role in one of his films.

Neither man signed the deal.

Explosive Article And The Fall
In November 2017, unhappy with the results she was getting, Charlotte turned to the press. She sent a message to The Hollywood Reporter and told them about her affair with Kevin, along with the promises that were made.

Staff from the industry trade reached out to Warner Brothers. Kevin vehemently denied the claims. He also threatened to sue anyone who printed a word of the story. His affair stayed secret for a bit longer.

Less than a year after the tip to The Hollywood Reporter, an anonymous note was sent to the CEO of WarnerMedia. There were claims that Kevin abused his position to go to bed with a young actress. He promised her roles, the message claimed.

An outside legal firm conducted an investigation. No evidence turned up, and Kevin was cleared of any wrongdoing. Charlotte fumed that nothing seemed to be breaking her way and that her former lover kept dodging any scandal.

She sent The Hollywood Reporter screenshots of her messages with Brett and Kevin in early 2019. This time, the former studio head would not be able to weasel out of the controversy. Two weeks after the piece was published, Kevin was let go from Warner Brothers.

Charlotte sued to vacate a gag order that had been placed on her. In her lawsuit, she claimed that Kevin raped her after doing a massive amount of cocaine. James Packer blocked her from leaving the room and offered her $30,000 to have sex with the other man. She refused. Her then-boyfriend stayed in the doorway and menaced her. Eventually, she went to bed with Kevin.

Later, she learned that James and Brett signed a nearly half a billion-dollar deal with Warner Brothers and that she was used to secure the deal.

Truths Will Out
In response to his ex's claims, James Packer released a statement refuting everything. All he wanted to do was help Charlotte succeed in her career and thought they broke up on good terms.

As the war of words between Kevin, James, and Charlotte began to enthrall the entertainment industry insiders, Brett worried that everyone's career could be damaged. Help arrived in the form of Hollywood fixer and executive extraordinaire, NBCUniversal vice chairman Ron Meyer.

Ron was known in Hollywood as someone who could solve problems. Often, he would bring two warring factions together in some peaceful solution. Or, in some cases, he would help competitors sign deals with talent.

With this group, Ron set up a mediation session. He believed they could air their grievances and preserve what little dignity they had left.

By the time she met Ron, Charlotte had a new boyfriend. She began dating director Neil Marshall as the rest of the drama played out.

A familiar scenario played out when she met Ron. They began hooking up and keeping their relationship secret. She pushed him for roles in Universal movies and NBC television shows. He declined to help her land roles within his studio.

Charlotte came to a settlement with James, Brett, and Kevin. They agreed to pay her $3 million over two years and finance Neil's new movie to serve as a star vehicle for her. In exchange, she would drop the war she had waged against them.

Ron Meyer would soon learn an important lesson; what happens in the dark is revealed in the light.

Careers Derailed and Destroyed
One August afternoon Ron Meyer ate lunch with Jeff Shell. This was not unusual; the men got along and often talked business together. However, this lunch was altogether different.

Ron told his friend that he cheated on his wife. He then revealed that his mistress's boyfriend was blackmailing him. Steve listened intently and then told the other man that he would need to resign to protect the organization.

Five days later, Ron released a statement that he was resigning from NBCUniversal. He acknowledged that he has been unfaithful to his wife. Then a bomb was dropped; he had been blackmailed by someone close to his former lover.

Soon after the announcement, another lawsuit was filed. James, Kevin, and Brett filed a civil extortion case against Charlotte. They claim she launched a shakedown to pad her pockets and threatened to bring them to ruin when they wouldn't pay her. A lawyer for the actress says their claims are false and lies.

There is also a lawsuit against Ron. Neil and Charlotte brought it against him for failing to provide funds for a movie with them. They believe he made a verbal contract saying he would, but money for the film never materialized. The lawsuit requests millions in damages and the money that they feel he promised to make the movie. Ron's lawyer has filed a motion to dismiss the case as frivolous.

Charlotte and Neil's movie that came from her original settlement has stalled. Neil was accused of stealing money from the film to buy a Ferrari, an allegation he denies.

Charlotte's dream of fame has come true. But at what cost?

Printed in Great Britain
by Amazon

57064537R00068